CONTENTS

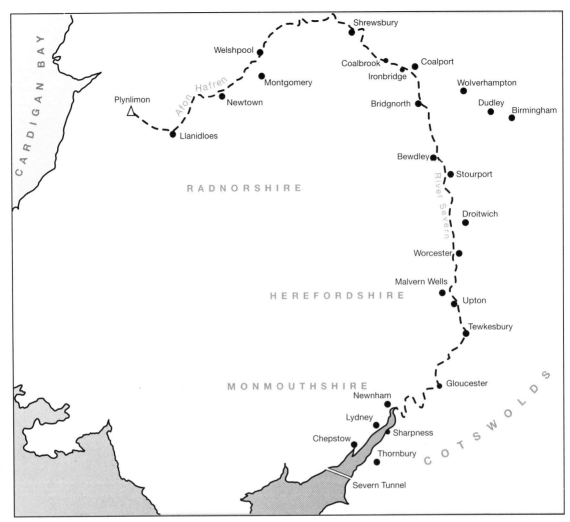

The course of the River Severn from source to sea.

A good ascent of old 'Father Plynlimon' may be made from Llanidloes, and in the course of it the source of the Severn can be visited. The 'origin' of the river has been told in legends grave and gay, lively and severe. Ours is a homely one, and perhaps as trustworthy as others that are more ambitious. It is that three little rivers slept in a hole on the mountain, and one evening they agreed to set off the next morning to seek their fortunes, and their father, old Plynlimon, promised them as a dowry all the land they could cover in a day's journey. The *Severn* got up first, and after making a short spurt eastward spied the *Wye* following, so she darted off to the south. The *Rheidol*, who got up last, took the conduct of her sisters so much to heart that she dashed headlong to the sea, and speedily committed suicide at Aberystwyth.

(Askew Roberts, *The Gossiping Guide to Wales*, Hodder & Stoughton, 1877)

A Postcard
from the
Severn

Jan Dobrzynski & Keith Turner

SUTTON PUBLISHING

First published in 2006 by
Sutton Publishing Limited · Phoenix Mill
Thrupp · Stroud · Gloucestershire GL5 2BU

The lines from *A Shropshire Lad* on p. 46 are reproduced by kind permission of The Society of Authors as the Literary Representative of the Estate of A.E. Housman.

British Library Cataloguing in Publication Data
A catalogue record for this book is available from the British Library.

ISBN 0-7509-4222-3

Typeset in 10.5/13.5pt Photina
Typesetting and origination by
Sutton Publishing Limited.
Printed and bound in England by
J.H. Haynes & Co. Ltd, Sparkford.

INTRODUCTION

Flowing 220 miles from the slopes of Plynlimon near Cardigan Bay to the Bristol Channel, the Severn is the mightiest of British rivers. Known to the Romans as Sabrina, and to the Welsh as Afon Hafren, it has for centuries been a source of food and employment, a boundary, a barrier, a trade route, a place of leisure and quiet enjoyment, a haven for wildlife and an inspiration for artists and writers. It has been crossed by fords and ferries, bridged over and tunnelled under, canalised in places and left untouched in others; it has been witness to the very beginnings of culture in the British Isles, to invasion and to battle, and to the birth of the Industrial Revolution that shaped the world in which we live.

This is the story of the Severn, a story that falls naturally into five chapters corresponding to the five different, distinctive landscapes through which the river flows. It is in the nature of things that a river as long as the Severn, during its journey to the sea, will undergo a number of significant transformations. The initial trickle from its source in bog or spring will, as it gathers pace, quickly become a fast-flowing stream, though narrow enough to be crossed in one bound. Soon, however, it widens as it gathers more water from its valley and presents rather more of an obstacle, and that single leap has to be replaced by a succession of jumps from one stepping stone to another. Simple bridges now appear and, as the river broadens further, fording points are established where its bed is hard enough, and its level low enough, to allow the safe passage of foot-travellers, livestock and vehicles.

The river has entered its middle age, occupying the wide valley it has carved for itself from the surrounding landscape over countless millennia. Swollen by a myriad of tributary ditches and streams, it is now deep enough to carry commercial vessels: passing the upper limit of navigation it becomes a trading highway linked to the sea, to canals and to other navigable rivers, and lined with quays and warehouses; gone are the fords and simple one-arched bridges, replaced by ferries, and by spans of increasing technological complexity high enough not to hinder the passage of the all-important boats beneath them. Finally, the river enters its old age as it nears the sea. Broad, serene and tidal in nature, it passes its lowest bridging point and widens even further into its estuary, merging seamlessly with the sea.

The story of the Severn begins in a peat bog at Blaenhafren, at 1,968ft above sea level on the eastern slopes of the mountainous dome of Plynlimon a little to the east of Aberystwyth; here, less than 2 miles to the south, the Afon Gwy (in English, the River Wye) also rises, destined – somewhat astonishingly – to join the Severn at the end of both rivers' journeys. From Plynlimon the mountain stream that is the young Afon Hafren flows for some 10 miles in a generally south-easterly direction through a mixture of open countryside, forest, rocky gorges, rapids and waterfalls, to the market town of Llanidloes, where it meets the A470; from here on to the sea the river will be closely paralleled for virtually its entire length by either road or railway, the builders of these other two great trading highways taking advantage of the comparatively level valley floor so thoughtfully smoothed out for them by the river. Swinging north-eastwards through Newtown and Welshpool, the river leaves the land of its birth behind when it crosses the English border just before reaching Shrewsbury. Here it becomes the River Severn, looping around the ancient fortified town in almost a complete circle before heading south-east through the lush, cattle-fattening country of the Marches and on past the landscape-dominating volcanic plug known as the Wrekin.

The Severn is now heading for its section of greatest historical importance: the Ironbridge Gorge, birthplace of the Industrial Revolution; officially designated by UNESCO as a World Heritage Site, today it justifiably attracts tourists from around the globe. The spectacular landscape of the gorge left behind, the picturesque town of Bridgnorth is reached, now the home of the Severn Valley Railway, perhaps the most famous of England's preserved steam lines. Now the river enters its most unspoilt stretch as it exchanges the Shropshire hills for the gentler countryside of Worcestershire, passing a succession of villages and small towns on its way to Worcester. Today the river is navigable from Stourport down to Worcester and beyond, and can be accessed by narrowboats from the national canal network; the old commercial craft may be long vanished, but their place has been filled by pleasure boats a-plenty.

At Tewkesbury, the Warwickshire Avon joins the Severn from the east and, though still a long way from the sea, the enlarged river was once tidal from this point onwards but, since various major alterations to the Severn were made downstream at Gloucester to aid navigation, the twice-daily fluctuations in the water level above them are not as noticeable today. And so on to Chepstow, on the western bank of the river, where it is joined by the Wye in a confluence of waters half a mile wide. Here, in 1966, a new lowest bridging point on the river was established with the opening of the Severn Bridge carrying the M4 (now the M48) across both the Severn and the Wye – and this was itself superseded in 1996 when the Second Severn Bridge, carrying the re-routed M4, was opened.

It is perhaps fitting to end this journey down one of Britain's great trading routes of the past with a nod to an even older type of highway. In 1997 the long-distance footpath known as the Severn Way was completed, providing an uninterrupted, waymarked walking trail beside the river; linking with a number of local and regional paths, it runs for 210 miles from the source of the river to Severn Beach on the east side of the estuary by the Second Severn Bridge.

Details of the course of each section of the Severn Way, in relation to the river, can be found at the beginning of each chapter, and after the captions as appropriate (with mileages from the source).
All the postcards included in this book are from the authors' collections. Publication details are given at the end of the captions, if and as they appear on the cards.

1

A Welsh River

The Welsh portion of the Severn, under the name of the
Hafryn, first assumes noteworthy properties at Llanidloes,
one of the smaller Montgomeryshire towns.
(The Severn Valley, Great Western Railway, 2nd edn, 1923)

The Severn Way begins at Tarddiad Afon Hafren, the precisely marked source of the river, accessible on foot from the car park in the picnic area at Rhyd-y-Benwch in the Hafren Forest, 3 miles along the trail. From the car park the Way continues to follow the river closely to the town of Llanidloes (11¾ miles), principally on its northern bank.

(H.B.)

Here, in Powys in mid-Wales, gathered from the rain falling on the desolate slopes of Plynlimon, the Afon Hafren begins its long journey to the sea. (*Unidentified*)

As the Hafren approaches Llanidloes, the first town on its course, the mountainous landscape of its birth changes gradually but noticeably into rolling hills and pasture, and it is soon joined by two other youthful rivers: the Afon Dulas from the south and the Afon Clywedog from the north. (*Exclusive Sepiatone Series, The Photochrom Co. Ltd, London and Tunbridge Wells*)

Llanidloes is a small market town noted for its timber-framed Market Hall of *c.* 1600, now a local history museum, with its open ground floor. The town's name translates as 'the Church of St Idloes', a building that dates back to the fourteenth century – though on a far older religious site. (*Rogers Real Photographic Series, Llanidloes*)

Llanidloes from Penybank.

TOWN HALL & GREAT OAK STREET, LLANIDLOES.

Llanidloes' principal thoroughfare, Great Oak Street, is shown, with the impressive Town Hall on the right. With the local government reorganisation of 1974 the old Welsh county of Montgomeryshire, within which the Hafren flows during its entire journey through the principality, became part of present-day Powys. (*Valentine & Sons*)

After Llanidloes the Severn Way makes a series of large detours to the north, rarely approaching the river again until Newtown (29¼ miles) is reached, where it crosses to the south bank.

Newtown is the next town encountered by the Hafren. Despite its name, the town received its Charter as long ago as 1279, when it was founded by Edward I, next to a ford across the river, to control a major land route between England and Wales. It has long been an important market town for the area and was once, as 'the Leeds of Wales', the centre of a sizeable flannel industry – the word 'flannel' probably derives from the Welsh for wool, *gwlan*, itself derived from the Latin *lana*. (*'Sepiatype' Postcard, Valentine & Sons Ltd, Dundee and London*)

Newtown – Drenewydd in Welsh – is here seen from the hills above the old hand-loom weaving quarter of Penygloddfa, looking southwards along Crescent Street towards Broad Street. In the centre distance by the railway station is the large Royal Welsh Warehouse, built by Sir Pryce Pryce-Jones in 1859 to house the world's first mail-order business. The tower of St David's Church, built in 1847, can be seen on the outskirts of the town on the right. (*RB Ltd, posted 1905*)

Newtown High Street is shown, looking towards the Cross Building, now a bank, supporting the Town Clock that commemorates Queen Victoria's 1897 Diamond Jubilee. Also here is the birthplace museum devoted to the social reformer and founder of the Co-operative movement, Robert Owen (1771–1858), who is buried at (the now ruined) St Mary's Church beside the river. (*RB Ltd*)

The ancient ford across the Hafren at Newtown was eventually replaced by a wooden bridge which, in 1826, gave way to an iron bridge built to the design of Thomas Penson. Known as Long Bridge, it stands at the end of Broad Street and is one of several by Penson, the County Surveyor, in former Montgomeryshire. ('*Park for People' Series, Park, Newtown, posted 1904*)

The Severn Way passes under the Long Bridge, then crosses the river on a footbridge known as the Halfpenny Bridge.

The first grand residence passed by the river is Powis Castle, standing high to the west of the Hafren just before Welshpool is reached. Dating from the thirteenth century but greatly altered and extended at various times since, it was bequeathed to the National Trust in 1952 by the fourth Earl of Powis, upon his death. (*Unidentified, posted 1906*)

After Newtown the Severn Way again detours north away from the river, this time to follow the route of the 1821 Montgomery Canal from Newtown until it rejoins the river the other side of Welshpool.

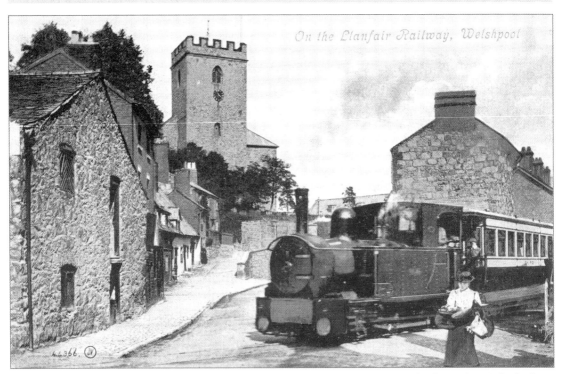

Between 1903 and 1956 the mainline railway yard at Welshpool station, beside the Hafren (which skirts the eastern side of the town), housed the Welshpool terminus of the 2ft 6in-gauge Welshpool & Llanfair Light Railway; from there it ran westwards through the town centre – as seen here shortly after opening – on the start of its 9½-mile journey to the village of Llanfair Caereinion. Built to serve the local agricultural community, it operates today as a preserved steam railway – still with its two original locomotives – though sadly it has proved impossible to reinstate this section through the streets. (*Valentine's Series, posted 1908*)

The Severn Bridge at Welshpool – Y Trallwng in Welsh – carries the A458 to Shrewsbury. (*Exclusive Sepiatone Series, The Photochrom Co. Ltd, London and Tunbridge Wells*)

The Severn Way is still a few hundred yards to the west, on the old canal towpath. It rejoins the Severn 2 miles further on at a spot known as Pool Quay (47 miles) in the Vale of Powis, where goods were once transshipped between barge and boat, this being the highest point of commercial navigation on the river at any time.

Breidden Hill, 6½ miles north-east of Welshpool and the highest (at 1,202ft) of the dramatic range known as the Breidden Hills (or the Breiddin), can be climbed along forest tracks and paths that start between the village of Criggion and its neighbouring quarry. The Hills can be seen for miles from the river to the west, and from Offa's Dyke crossing it close by. At the summit stands Admiral Rodney's Pillar alongside the earthworks of an Iron Age fort. ('*Cleveland*' *Series, R.M. & S. Ltd*)

Admiral Rodney's Pillar was erected on Breidden Hill in tribute to Montgomeryshire for the timber it supplied to build ships for the Royal Navy during the Napoleonic Wars, though is now as much a tribute to Admiral Rodney (1719–92) and his exploits – including his 1782 defeat of the French off Dominica – as a memorial to the county. A rather different tribute to Rodney stands by the road below the hill on the outskirts of Criggion: the Admiral Rodney – formerly Rodney's Pillar – public house. (*Wilding & Son Ltd, Shrewsbury, posted 1911*)

After passing east of here, the Severn Way again leaves the river on a northern detour, until reaching England just before Montford Bridge.

2

Into the Marches

It is close to this point that the Severn, now a 'goodly
river', both as regards the volume of its waters and the
beauty of the scenery on either bank, enters Shropshire.
(*The Severn Valley*, Great Western Railway, 2nd edn, 1923)

Rejoining the river at Montford Bridge (63½ miles), but only to cross it, the
Severn Way heads straight for Shrewsbury (70¼ miles) while the river twists
and turns in great loops towards the same destination. It then follows the
riverside through the town and out to Atcham (78½ miles) before leaving it
again, rejoining at Cressage.

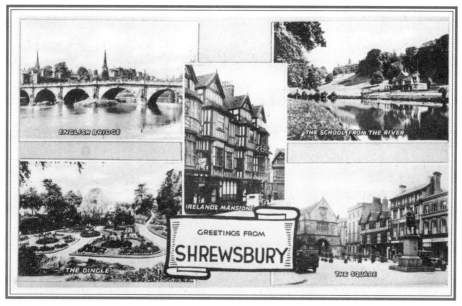

(*The Photochrom Co. Ltd, Tunbridge Wells*)

Crossing the border into England, the Afon Hafren becomes the River Severn and, to the west of Shrewsbury, meanders through woods and grasslands close to Preston Montford Hall, a Queen Anne country house – now a field study centre offering professional training and leisure courses on the environment. (*Unidentified*)

The old London to Holyhead road, the A5, crossed the Severn at Montford Bridge 4 miles north-west of Shrewsbury, the village taking its name from the original medieval bridge here. This was replaced in 1792 by one designed by Thomas Telford; the road in this view disappears over the bridge in the distance, after passing the Wingfield Arms Inn. (*Wilding & Son Ltd, Shrewsbury*)

Telford (1757–1834) designed seven Severn bridges, this one at Montford being the first. Besides being a natural bridging point on the river, the site was, in ancient times, a convenient meeting place for the Welsh and English leaders to conduct negotiations throughout their centuries of intermittent armed conflict. In 1283, the captive Dafydd ap Gruffudd, the last true Prince of Wales, was handed over here by his countrymen; sentenced to death by King Edward I, he was hanged, drawn and quartered in Shrewsbury. (*Unidentified*)

And so the river enters Shrewsbury, doubling back on itself from the north to flow almost due west as it begins its great loop of more than 180 degrees around the old town centre. There are two ancient bridges here: the Welsh Bridge on the north side of the old town, and the English Bridge to the south-east. The present Welsh Bridge, seen here, was built in 1795 by Messrs Tilly & Carline – seemingly with some 'borrowing' of design from Telford's Montford Bridge – at a cost of £8,000; it is 266ft in length. The difference in river width, and hence bridge length, between the two sites is also noticeable. (*Valentine's XL Series*)

The Welsh Bridge is shown again, seen from further on round the river's great bend. The rope-worked ferry is no more, replaced in 1922 by the Port Hill Bridge, a suspension footbridge linking the district of that name on the north bank with Quarry Park on the other. A plaque on the bridge commemorates its erection by the Shropshire Horticultural Society, Port Hill residents and the engineers, David Rowell & Co. Ltd of Westminster. (*The Woodbury Series, posted 1911*)

The Port Hill Bridge takes the Severn Way over the river here, to the townside bank, on which it then remains until the district of Monkmoor is reached on the north-eastern side of Shrewsbury, where it crosses over on the road bridge to what is now the west bank.

The Boat House Inn, centre, once used to house seventeenth-century plague victims, still stands beside the Port Hill Bridge, though this view was captured long before the ferry was replaced. Note the boats for hire on the river, this comparatively broad and placid section of the Severn being an ideal place for leisure boating – and competitive rowing. (*The British Mirror Series, posted 1907*)

A timeless view of this stretch of the Severn is shown, with Quarry Park on the left and the Grammar School in the distance. (*Unidentified, posted 1903*)

For over a century the Shrewsbury Horticultural Society has held an annual flower show in Quarry Park, beside the river, with the central, sunken gardens known as the Dingle providing the centrepiece for the two-day event. Looking towards the north-east, the 150ft-high cupola of St Chad's Church can be seen protruding above the trees. (*Valentine's 'Colourtone' Series*)

The Dingle, with its magnificently well-kept gardens and pristine flower borders, now as then. (*Celesque Series, The Photochrom Co. Ltd, London and Tunbridge Wells*)

BALLOON ASCENT, SHREWSBURY FLOWER SHOW.

The Shrewsbury Flower Show has also been an occasion for more spectacular entertainment, and in its early years tethered balloon flights above the park were a regular event. However, their popularity later declined, no doubt hastened by an incident in 1906 when a balloon broke free and took its passengers on a hair-raising 25-mile journey to Staffordshire! (*Livesey & Co. Ltd, Shrewsbury*)

St Chad's Church replaced a Saxon church, in Belmont in the town centre, destroyed in 1788 when its tower collapsed on to it. It was not rebuilt, but an alternative site was chosen for a new church above Quarry Park. Designed by Scottish architect George Steuart, it incorporates a mixture of Doric and Corinthian architectural styles in the interior and façade. Consecrated on 19 August 1792, it features magnificent David Evans stained-glass windows and, most unusually, a 100ft-diameter circular nave. (*Unidentified*)

Shrewsbury prospered during the Middle Ages, principally in the wool and leather industries: the Domesday Book of 1086 lists 252 houses in the town and by the fourteenth century poll tax returns show a population of some three thousand. Reflecting this growth and prosperity, a new Market Hall was built in 1596 in the town centre for the use of wool merchants and drapers; today it has been sympathetically restored and is now a prestigious film and digital media centre showing films from all over the world. The statue in front is of the soldier and statesman Robert Clive (1725–74), better known as Clive of India. After his service in the East India Company he became MP for Shrewsbury and in 1762 was elected Lord Mayor. His son Edward (1754–1839) was given the title Earl of Powis in 1804, so strengthening his link (by marriage) to Powis Castle. (*Valentine's Series, posted 1909*)

The gateway leading to the courthouse of the Marcher Lords – Norman barons holding land in Wales and on the border (the Marches). Since the Marches were not subject to the same laws as England, the Lords had their own court, held successively at Ludlow and Shrewsbury; eventually their lands were seized by the Crown and given to more loyal – and trustworthy – nobles. (*Unidentified, posted 1905*)

Below: The gatehouse, which dates from 1620, is shown from the other side. (*Frith's Series, F. Frith & Co. Ltd, Reigate, posted 1912*)

Irelands Mansion
Shrewsbury

Shrewsbury became even more prosperous during the reign of the Tudors, and wealthy citizens erected high-status half-timbered buildings, many of which are still standing. Ireland's Mansion is an impressive black-and-white house in the High Street close to the Market Hall, built as the town residence of the Ireland family of Albrighton. (*Unidentified*)

Opposite: Wyle Cop, meaning 'ridge top', developed as part of the busy London to Holyhead road, leads down from the High Street to the English Bridge. Henry, Earl of Richmond, is said to have stayed in the house on the right after the town surrendered to his army on 15 August 1485, the day before he made his way to Bosworth Field in Leicestershire to defeat King Richard III, take the crown as King Henry VII and put an end to the Wars of the Roses. (*Unidentified*)

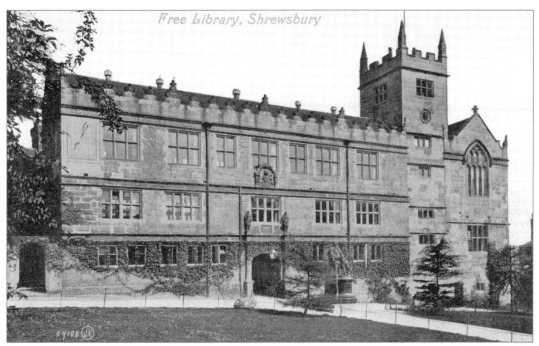

Charles Robert Darwin (1809–82), the exponent of evolution by natural selection, was born in Shrewsbury and, with his brother Erasmus, attended the Grammar School from September 1818. The school still stands in Castle Street, opposite the Council House Gatehouse, and now houses the town's public library; the bronze statue is of the seated Darwin. Founded by Edward VI in 1552, the Grammar School superseded the monastic colleges of Shrewsbury Abbey, St Chad's and St Mary's ended by the Dissolution of the Monasteries; by 1630 the whole complex of master's house, chapel, library and schoolrooms was substantially complete. (*Valentine's Series, posted 1912*)

The Church of St Mary the Virgin, along with the original St Chad's, was the most important church in Shrewsbury at the time of the Norman Conquest. From *c.* 1150 to 1477 it underwent continual development, culminating in the building of the 138ft West Tower (said to be the third tallest in England). Standing at the highest spot in the town, it dominates the local skyline. Today St Mary's survives as Shrewsbury's only complete medieval church with its impressive stained-glass windows and carvings. (*L. Wilding, The Salop Art Press, Shrewsbury*)

FISH STREET AND ST. JULIAN'S CHURCH, SHREWSBURY.

One of the many delights of Shrewsbury is the number of surviving narrow medieval thoroughfares in the town, with their associated alleyways known as shuts. This is Fish Street, behind the High Street, looking towards St Julian's Church; fish were sold here before the general market opened in 1869. The steps where the children are sitting are Bear Steps, so named from the former Bear Inn on the corner. (*Unidentified*)

Shrewsbury's status as a town of importance, along with confidence in its defences, led to a royal mint being established in the town centre by the time of Alfred the Great. The production of coins in the town ceased in 1272, and the remains of the mint have been all but obliterated by successive building developments since then. (*Valentine's XL Series*)

School Lane, Shrewsbury.

School Lane once ran the full length of the south wing and in front of the main entrance of the old Grammar School, joining the thoroughfare known as Castle Gates by the corner of the west wing. In 1825 road improvements to Castle Gates prompted the headmaster to close part of the lane and convert it into the school playground. A porter's lodge and gates were built at the top of the lane the following year. (*L. Wilding, The Salop Art Press, Shrewsbury, posted 1907*)

Shrewsbury from Grammar School

As the county town of Shropshire, or Salop, Shrewsbury has long outgrown the original confines of its sandstone peninsula within the Severn's loop. Here the old town is seen from the more modern, south-western suburb of Kingsland, reached by the Kingsland Bridge on the far right. (*Valentine's Series*)

School Ferry and Schools, Shrewsbury

Shrewsbury Grammar School moved across the river to Kingsland in July 1882, undoubtedly helping the neighbourhood become a wealthy Victorian suburb. The new school is seen here dominating the skyline, above the rope-worked school ferry which once connected Quarry Place, and the town, to Kingsland. The school boat club was founded in 1866, with a boathouse next to the Prince of Wales public house shared with the Pengwern club, though by 1881 the school had acquired the pub and rebuilt the boathouse. A new boathouse was built in 1921 as a memorial to the school's old boys who fell in the First World War. (*Valentine's Series, posted 1904*)

The ferry is shown in action, on an official promotional issue for the London & North Western Railway, the company that had its own line from Crewe to the town. On the reverse of the card the virtues of Shrewsbury are proclaimed thus: 'No inland holiday resort in the Kingdom can excel in the unique attractions possessed by Shrewsbury, and few towns in England are so rich in historical buildings and other relics of antiquity, both secular and ecclesiastical.' (*McCorquodale & Co. Limited, posted 1910*)

Pengwern Boat Club took its name from the early Saxon kingdom of the area – its capital, Llys Pengwern, eventually became Shrewsbury – to distinguish itself from the Shrewsbury Rowing Club already in existence. After sharing the school's boathouse, it purchased its own site in 1881 and moved to a new clubhouse a little upriver; both premises can be seen in this view. The New Bridge referred to in the caption is Kingsland Bridge, in the distance. (*Valentine's Series*)

The imposing 1881 Pengwern boathouse was built when the club outgrew its shared premises – by this date competitive rowing was becoming a popular means of exercise as well as a pastime for young Victorian gentlemen. (*Unidentified*)

The two boathouses can be seen from the opposite, downriver, perspective – from Kingsland Bridge in fact – with the school ferry captured in mid-stream. (*Unidentified, posted 1906*)

The Boathouse, Shrewsbury.

Pengwern boathouse is shown again at a slightly later date, after some remodelling to the steps and gardens had been carried out. The verdant area where the boathouses stand is known as Beck's Field. ('*Princess Series*', *R.M. & S. Ltd, Shrewsbury*)

In 1882 – the same year the Grammar School relocated – the Kingsland Bridge Co. built this elegant single-span iron bridge across the Severn to link the old town with the suburb of Kingsland, sounding the death knell for the ferry. (*Boots the Chemist*)

Kingsland Bridge, with a span of 212ft, was, like many of the Severn bridges, built as a toll bridge; it is unusual for retaining that status today. ('*Cleveland Series*', *R.M. & S. Ltd, Shrewsbury*)

Greyfriars footbridge opened in 1880, two years before Kingsland Bridge (just out of sight upstream round the bend in the river), its deck supported from two lattice girder suspension towers standing on concrete piers. The reason for its construction was that the English Bridge (behind the camera) was often snarled with traffic and the new bridge relieved some of the pedestrian congestion on its narrow footpaths. (*Valentine's Series*)

A very early card shows the English Bridge as it appeared at the end of the nineteenth century; it was designed by Shrewsbury architect John Gwynn (1713–86) and built in 1769–74 at the immense cost of £15,710. There has been a crossing over the Severn at this point since the early twelfth century, between Wyle Cop and Shrewsbury Abbey; bridge construction was aided by a small but very conveniently placed island in the middle of the river. (*Raphael Tuck & Sons*)

THE OLD ENGLISH BRIDGE, SHREWSBURY.

A slightly later view of the English Bridge which, as built, was 400ft long with a central arch 60ft wide and 40ft high. Unfortunately, the thoroughfare across it was only 25ft in width, leading to increasing congestion until 1925–7, when it was partially dismantled and rebuilt as the wider, flatter structure that exists today. (*L. Wilding, The Salop Art Press, Shrewsbury, posted 1908*)

Roger de Montgomery founded Shrewsbury's Benedictine abbey in 1083; although the abbey church was almost totally destroyed at the Dissolution of the Monasteries by King Henry VIII, the nave, north porch and western tower survived to be incorporated into the parish church, resulting in a rather unusual-looking building. This is its western end, with a large Perpendicular window immediately above a Norman doorway. In recent years the abbey has become famous as the home of author Ellis Peters' fictional detective monk, Brother Cadfael, with the popular television series based on her books attracting many visitors to the site. (*The Milton 'Photogravure' Series, Woolstone Bros, London*)

A railway station once occupied part of the site of the abbey, with an old pulpit, somewhat bizarrely, standing at the end of one of the platforms! The station was the terminus of the independent Potteries, Shrewsbury & North Wales Railway – known affectionately as the 'Potts' – which ran north-westwards to Llanymynech; it later became, as the Shropshire & Montgomeryshire Light Railway, part of Colonel Stephens' light railway empire. The railway has long since rusted away, and Abbey Foregate station is all but forgotten, but the pulpit still stands witness to an earlier monastic age. (*Unidentified*)

Lord Hill's Column, Shrewsbury.

This statue of Lord Rowland Hill (1772–1842), whose family seat was Hawkstone Park in the north of the county, stands on what is believed to be the tallest Doric column in the world (133ft), opposite the Shirehall on the eastern edge of Shrewsbury. It was erected in 1814–16 to commemorate his valour and leadership he displayed in the Peninsular War and at the Battle of Waterloo. (*Wilding & Son Ltd, Shrewsbury*)

Beyond the English Bridge a pleasant riverside path leads to Shrewsbury Castle; the walkway forms part of Route 81 of the National Cycle Network, beginning at the Quarry and connecting Shrewbury with Wellington via a series of country lanes, quiet roads and dedicated cycleways. The castle watchtower on the skyline is known as Laura's Tower, and was added by Thomas Telford in 1787. (*Valentine's Series*)

Shrewsbury Castle stands high on the narrow neck of land formed by the great loop of the Severn around the old town. It has been a fortified site since the Dark Ages and when, in 778, the Saxon king of Mercia captured the rival kingdom of Pengwern, the town of Scrobbesbyrig was founded where Llys Pengwern had been, the name evolving with time into 'Shrewsbury'. This is the castle from the landward side, close to the entrance to the railway station. (*Valentine's Series, posted 1908*)

Given its geographical location, it is not surprising that Shrewsbury developed as an important railway centre in the nineteenth century, with seven distinct routes into the town worked by a number of railway companies which, quite quickly, amalgamated or merged into the Great Western Railway and the London & North Western Railway. Built by a consortium of companies and opened in 1849 as Shrewsbury General, the town's mock-Tudor main station stands at the junction of Castle Street and Castle Gates, with its platforms actually spanning the Severn. (*Raphael Tuck & Sons' 'Town and City' Series*)

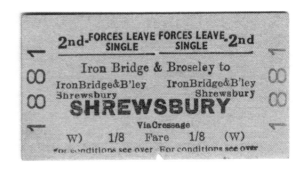

Shrewsbury railway ephemera: a GWR luggage label of the type that once adorned millions of passengers' trunks and suitcases, and a British Railways (Western Region) special-issue ticket to the town from Iron Bridge & Broseley via Cressage – all places on the Severn.

After the Norman Conquest Roger de Montgomery was granted the earldom of Shropshire and made Shrewsbury his centre, beginning construction of the first motte and bailey stronghold in 1070, in wood. The next century saw it rebuilt in stone, while in the thirteenth century a stone wall for the town was added. After the English Civil Wars in the seventeenth century it fell derelict until it was rebuilt by Telford in the 1780s as a residence for the local MP, Sir William Pulteney. Now, as the Shropshire Regimental Museum, it houses the collections of four Shropshire regiments. A rank of horse-cabs awaits passengers from the station. (*The British Mirror Series, posted 1908*)

After leaving Shrewsbury the Severn swings south-eastwards, passing Haughmond Hill on its left, where one of the county's most impressive ruins can be found: Haughmond Abbey. Formerly an Augustinian house dating from the early twelfth century, in 1403 it was witness to the Battle of Shrewsbury close by, when King Henry IV defeated a rebellion led by the Earl of Northumberland, and at which Northumberland's son Henry Percy – the famous Harry Hotspur – was killed. (*Unidentified*)

Atcham village lies 4 miles south-east of Shrewsbury by the entrance to Attingham Park, the former home of the Hill family and now a National Trust property. Almost hidden behind the trees in this view is the eleventh-century parish church of St Eata beside the old A5 road bridge over the Severn. Parts of the church date back to Saxon times and stone taken from the nearby Roman city of Viroconium has been identified in its walls. (*Wilding & Son Ltd, Shrewsbury*)

Built between 1772 and 1779, this bridge at Atcham was designed by John Gwynn, architect of the English Bridge in Shrewsbury. (His third Severn bridge, at Worcester, appears later.) The bridge, believed to be the third on the site since medieval times, cost £8,630 to construct and was built by Gwynn himself after the original contractor proved unsatisfactory; it has seven spans and a length of 407ft and is a very close copy of the one at Shrewsbury. In 1924 the County Council decided to replace it, but thankfully spared it and built the new one alongside. (*Mallinson Series*)

The New Atcham Bridge, Erected 1929

The new ferro-concrete bridge at Atcham, opened in 1929 to accommodate the substantial increase in traffic on the A5 trunk road; at 30ft, the carriageway is almost twice the width of that on Gwynn's bridge (which is now used by pedestrians). Since the opening of the Shrewsbury bypass and the shifting of the A5 to a new, northern alignment, the road through Atcham has become the B4380 and has experienced a welcome decrease in traffic volume. (*'Princess' Series, R.M. & S. Ltd, Shrewsbury*)

The Severn Way crosses the river here (78½ miles) from the west bank and takes a more direct course south-west to Cressage (84½ miles).

Attingham Park at Atcham, set in 250 acres of deer park landscaped by Humphry Repton, was constructed in 1783–5 for Noel Hill, the first Lord Berwick, as an encasing of Tern Hall, a modest Queen Anne house of 1701 which stands behind the new central block. Designed by George Steuart – also responsible for St Chad's Church in Shrewsbury – it is one of Shropshire's grandest houses, with a magnificent Regency interior. (*Unidentified*)

ATTINGHAM PARK   THE SHROPSHIRE ADULT COLLEGE

(*Photo: A. F. Kersting*)

ATTINGHAM PARK · SHREWSBURY

THE SOUTH FRONT
(*by George Steuart, 1785*)

Property of The National Trust   Shropshire Adult College

Designed as a neo-classical mansion reflecting the wealth and prestige of Lord Berwick, Attingham Park is now a National Trust property, having served time during the Second World War as a billet for airmen from Fighter Command based at Atcham, then for American airmen when that base was transferred to the USAAF. In 1947 it was bequeathed to the NT and the following year became an adult education college. (*Unidentified*)

VIROCONIUM. PASSAGE FROM WATLING STREET LEADING TO ROMAN BATHS.

A little over a mile to the east of Atcham, just north of the village of Wroxeter and overlooking the meandering course of the Severn, lie the remains of the Roman city of Viroconium. It was founded here, in the first century AD, as a garrison town to guard the river crossing and to serve as a base for operations against the local tribes. It lay on, and was supplied by, Watling Street, running from London to Chester, one of the great arterial roads laid down by the Romans to help subdue most of Britain. (*Wilding & Son Ltd, Shrewsbury*)

Following the Roman invasion of AD 43, Viroconium was established within a few years as a military stronghold to control primarily the Cornovii tribe, whose base was the Wrekin a few miles to the east, and Prince Caractacus of the Britons leading armed resistance from Wales to the west. By AD 58 the town was occupied by the Fourteenth Legion; when it was recalled to Rome eleven years later, garrison duties were taken on by the Twentieth Legion who remained until moved to Chester in AD 78. Viroconium then came under civil administration, growing over the next 300 years to become the fourth-largest Romano-British city in the country, boasting such institutions as a forum, a law court – and the obligatory grand public baths.

The city appears to have gone into decline during the decades after the Romans left Britain at the beginning of the fifth century, its inhabitants probably moving downhill towards the ford, so establishing the nearby village of Wroxeter, or decamping to Pengwern, or 'Knoll of Alders' – the embryonic Shrewsbury. What remained of the city was plundered as a source of building materials until, reduced to its foundations, it disappeared beneath shifting soil and encroaching vegetation for more than a thousand years.

The Severn Way passes between the river and both Viroconium and Wroxeter on its way to Cressage.

VIROCONIUM.

COLONADE OF FORUM FROM WATLING STREET.

'The gale, it plies the saplings double, It blows so hard, 'twill soon be gone: To-day the Roman and his trouble Are ashes under Uricon.' A.E. Housman, *A Shropshire Lad*, 1896. (*Wilding & Son Ltd, Shrewsbury*)

3

Through the Gorge

The County of China, Coal and Coracles
        (*The Severn Valley*, Great Western Railway, 2nd edn, 1923)

The Severn Way rejoins the river at Cressage (84½ miles), detours a little to the south, then rejoins to accompany it through the Ironbridge Gorge and on to Bridgnorth (99¼ miles) and beyond, thereafter keeping close to it for the rest of its course.

(Kingsway Real Photo Series, WHS)

The Wrekin from Cressage-Shropshire.

The stretch of the Severn before the Ironbridge Gorge is dominated by the looming presence of the Wrekin, the 1,335ft-high remnant of an ancient volcano. The next village of any size encountered by the river is Cressage, its name derived from the Cressage (originally Christ's) Oak, which stood where the war memorial now is and under which St Augustine is reputed to have addressed the bishops of Wales in 584. (*Unidentified*)

River Severn at Buildwas.

The ancient coracle (in Welsh, *cwrwgl*) was a common sight on the upper reaches of the Severn when this postcard was published; sadly it has all but disappeared and is seldom seen on the river today – a notable exception being in Shrewsbury where one has been employed for years to fish footballs out of the river when they are booted out of the club ground at Gay Meadow! This one-man portable boat, weighing 25–40lb, was traditionally made with a skin of calico waterproofed with pitch or tar over a hazel or willow frame. Extremely versatile, it could be used for line fishing, elver netting – or to avoid toll bridge charges. (*W.S. Allcock, Ironbridge, posted 1919*)

This romanticised landscape shows the ruins of Our Lady and St Chad's Abbey at Buildwas, below Cressage. It was founded in 1135 by Roger de Clinton, Bishop of Coventry and Lichfield, with the monks belonging to the Savignac order of the mother abbey at Furness, though in 1147 the order merged with the Cistercians. The abbey was relatively small and derived its income largely from charging tolls to cross the Severn. (*On the Severn Series, S. Hildersheimer & Co. Ltd, London & Manchester*)

The Severn Way rejoins the river immediately downstream of the abbey, crossing to the north bank on the A4169 road bridge.

Buildwas Abbey appears to have enjoyed a relatively peaceful history, apart from some troublesome Welsh raids and the murder of the abbot in 1342 by one of the monks, Thomas Tong. Monastic life continued until the Dissolution of the Monasteries in 1535 when its estate was given to Lord Powys; part of its library was saved and is now housed at Trinity College, Cambridge. The site is now an English Heritage property. (*L. Wilding, The Salop Art Press, Shrewsbury*)

A row of sturdy columns remains along the length of the nave of the abbey church. The chapter house, cloister buildings, a rib-vaulted crypt beneath the north transept and a sacristy are also well preserved, unaltered from the twelfth century. The infirmary also survives but has been converted into a house, now used as a social club by employees of the nearby Ironbridge Power Station. (*Unidentified*)

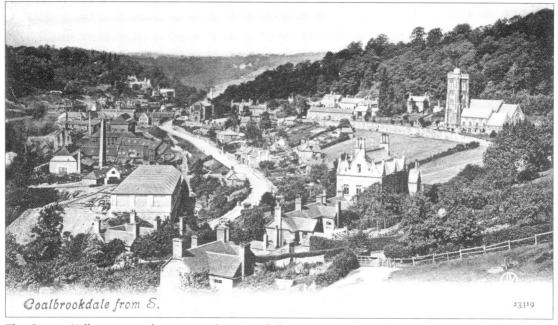

The Severn Valley now undergoes an abrupt and dramatic transformation as it enters the Ironbridge Gorge by the village of Coalbrookdale (the old name for the gorge). It was here, in 1709, that Abraham Darby started using coke instead of charcoal to smelt iron, a technological advance that literally sparked the Industrial Revolution, turning the gorge into the cradle of the industrial age. Today the village is home to the Museum of Iron, the Enginuity science and engineering exhibition and the Ironbridge Institute, among other attractions. (*Valentine's Series*)

Sir John Fowler (1817–98) designed the Albert Edward Bridge at Coalbrookdale as a sister to the Victoria Bridge at Arley (see p. 69), with the Coalbrookdale Iron Works casting its sections. When it opened in 1864 it carried the grandly named Much Wenlock, Craven Arms & Coalbrookdale Railway Co.'s line across the Severn to a junction with the Severn Valley Railway at Buildwas. The through routes of both the MWCA&CR and the adjoining section of the SVR were both closed in the early 1960s, though the bridge survives, used by coal trains to the sidings at Ironbridge Power Station, which lie beyond the embankment seen here from Benthall Edge. Today immense cooling towers and generator buildings take up much of this scene. (*Frith's Series, F. Frith & Co. Ltd, Reigate*)

The GWR's Severn Valley Railway station serves Ironbridge and Broseley, a few yards south of the famous iron bridge. A Swindon-built Armstrong 0–6–0 locomotive with its Shrewsbury-bound train waits between the level-crossing gates; at the opposite platform is a passing train, heading for Bridgnorth. (Bradshaw's railway timetables of this period show only one passing train scheduled during the day, the 12 noon weekday service.) Nothing remains of the station buildings today, as they were totally

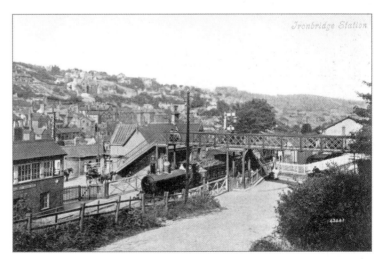

demolished after the line closed in 1963 and replaced by a car park. A few rails embedded in the road above the bridge, a level-crossing gatepost beside the old trackbed (now a footpath), and the Station Hotel stand silent witnesses to the former railway. (*Valentine's Series, posted 1905*)

Iron Bridge   *Erected by Coalbrookdale Company 1779.   The First Iron Bridge ever erected.*

This world-famous iron bridge across the Severn was cast, in sections, at Coalbrookdale by Abraham Darby III in 1777–9, making it the first single-span iron bridge of its size in the world; the town that grew up around it became known, not surprisingly, as Ironbridge. Designed by F.T. Pritchard to replace a ferry crossing, the bridge has a total length of 196ft with a central span of 100ft 6in and a rise of 50ft; each of the five main ribs, made up of two castings, is some 70ft long and weighs 5¾ tons. Even the 24ft-wide carriageway is made of cast-iron plates. In all, the total weight of the cast iron used is estimated at nearly 380 tons.

Formerly a toll bridge operated by the Ironbridge Bridge Co., it was closed to vehicles in the 1930s because of buckling caused by the movement of the river banks – always a problem along this stretch of the Severn – and was strengthened and restored four decades later in recognition of its importance, an importance that every year brings thousands of visitors to the gorge from all over the world. (*Valentine's Series, W.S. Allcock, Ironbridge*)

Opposite: This unusual perspective of the bridge gives a good idea of how high the central arch had to be built so that the sailing vessels upon which the prosperity of the gorge depended might pass under it unimpeded. The original tolls charged for crossing it varied according to the number of animals pulling the vehicle in question: 1s 6d for four, 1s for two and 6d for one. A footnote to the published table states, rather meanly, that 'This Bridge is private property, every Officer or Soldier, whether on duty or not, is liable to pay toll for passing over, as well as any luggage waggon, Mail-coach or the Royal Family.' (*Unidentified*)

> *The iron bridge is used by the Severn Way to take it back to the south bank of the river (90¼ miles).*

THE BRIDGE: BUILT A.D. 1779.   IRONBRIDGE. 89.

Ironbridge's former Market Hall, built in about 1790, stands almost opposite the approach to the bridge (behind the viewer). Today the building houses a post office, estate agent and shops – including 'Bears in the Square', from the window of which its soft-toy inhabitants look out on to a car park. The Tontine Hotel is on the left and an earlier Market Hall, seen here with its open ground floor bricked in on the right, is now a chemist's shop; a teashop and a public convenience have replaced the building seen between the two halls. (*Valentine's Series*)

Sadly, the buildings here in the centre and immediately on the left have been demolished to accommodate road widenings, and a traffic island stands in the middle of the scene while the cooling towers of Ironbridge Power Station rise in the distance against the wooded slopes of the gorge. Remarkably, the lamppost – cast at Coalbrookdale and erected by public subscription in 1898 – survives, relocated a few feet away. (*Valentine's Series*)

The Big Water Wheel, or the Great Wheel of Benthall, as it was sometimes called, was used to power a flourmill at Ironbridge. It stood beside the Benthall road but, sadly, was demolished in the 1930s. The mill ruins, however, remain. (*Valentine's Series*)

St Bartholomew's Church at Benthall was built in 1667 to replace one destroyed during the 1645 attack on the neighbouring Benthall Hall; an unusual feature is its vertical declining sundial above the door. The village lies just south of the Severn, to which it was linked by a tramroad in the eighteenth century and, as elsewhere in the gorge, was home to iron foundries and potteries. A speciality product of the area was the coarse earthenware beer mugs used in Severnside inns – several of which consequently bore the name 'Mug House'. (*W.S. Allcock, Ironbridge*)

APLEY HALL.   PUBLISHED AT THE POSTERN GATE, BRIDGNORTH

Leaving Ironbridge, the river swings slowly southwards; on its eastern bank stands Apley Hall in a wooded park of some 245 acres. The Whitmore family held the estate from 1572 and the Hall was built in 1811 for Thomas Whitmore, MP for Bridgnorth. Reputedly the largest and most expensive country house ever built in Britain, it is also famous for being the inspiration for P.G. Wodehouse's Blandings Castle. In return for land on the opposite side of the river, the Severn Valley Railway was required to throw a (private) chain bridge across the Severn to link the park with Linley station (which opened with the whole line in 1862). Five years later the estate was sold out of the family and, after closing as a public school in 1987, is once again a private residence. (*The Postern Gate, Bridgnorth*)

Below Apley Hall is the approach to Bridgnorth, looking northwards to High Rock, below which can be seen Bridgnorth pumping station. To the left of High Rock is a smaller sandstone outcrop, Pendlestone Rock, below which, and beside the Telford road on the riverbank is the curious Fort Pendlestone; this began life as a flourmill in the thirteenth century, was converted to an ironworks by Abraham Darby III, then became a carpet factory before conversion in 1854 to a neo-Gothic residence by William Whitmore of Apley Hall. The sender's birthday greetings message to 'Maudie' includes 'When this you see oh think of me? and let me see you up a tree'. (*Valentine's Series, posted 1904*)

Looking the other way from the previous card, to the town of Bridgnorth. The landing stage for rowboats is at the town's boat club, which disbanded in 1924 but re-formed through the efforts of Constable Bill Williams and Dr E.L. Rhodes in 1953, the 'new' boathouse being an old Nissen hut. The hut still stands, though new premises have been converted from a nearby maltings. ('*Princess' Series, R.M. & S. Ltd, Shrewsbury*)

Bridgnorth from the air, looking northwards, with the river bridge and church in the castle grounds prominent landmarks – both Thomas Telford structures. The low-lying riverside and the elevated hill-top neighbourhoods grew together, and are called Low Town and High Town respectively, the former developing around quays and dockyards where there was once a thriving boat-building industry along with ironworks, tanneries and carpet mills. (*Jas. T. Foxhall, Postern Gate, Bridgnorth*)

High Town was destroyed by fire in 1646 when Parliamentary forces laying siege to Bridgnorth bombarded it. The medieval parish church of St Leonard's was one of the casualties, the destruction compounded by the ammunition stored within it. It was, however, rebuilt and, now redundant as a church, is used as the main venue for the English Haydn Festival held in and around the town every spring. (*Valentine's Series*)

There has been a bridge across the Severn at Bridgnorth since medieval times, the last in the series being rebuilt by Thomas Telford in 1810; further alterations were also carried out in 1960, primarily to widen the carriageway. (*'Cleveland' Series, R.M. & S. Ltd, Shrewsbury*)

From Castle Walk in High Town, the view unfolds of Low Town and the Severn. On the east bank across the river the large brick building on the left was once a seed mill but is now an antique centre, and to this day the building at the left-hand end of the bridge has a large sign painted on its gable end advertising the seed merchant to all who cross the bridge. (*Valentine's Series*)

STONEWAY STEPS, BRIDGNORTH.   PHOTO BY T. BROMWICH

PUBLISHED AT THE POSTERN GATE, BRIDGNORTH

Stoneway Steps lead down from Waterloo Terrace in High Town to the Severn bridge. Nearly two hundred in number, 160yd in length and bounded by kerbs of ornate cast iron, they occupy a steep passage carved out of the sandstone outcrop. Halfway down is the Theatre on the Steps, home of a theatre company operating from a converted eighteenth-century Congregational chapel. The wrought-iron wall-braces are nicknamed 'Pope's spectacles' after their maker's factory. (*The Postern Gate, Bridgnorth*)

CASTLE HILL RAILWAY, BRIDGNORTH   32505.JV.

Since 1892 High Town and Low Town have been connected by a 201ft-long funicular –
the Castle Hill Railway – running in a cutting in the rock face overlooking the Severn.
This view of the line, taken not long after its opening, shows the railway's parallel
3ft 8½in-gauge tracks and its two cars each with its own attendant. (*Valentine's Series*)

CLIFF RAILWAY & RIVER, BRIDGNORTH.

Originally the Castle Hill Railway was operated on the counterbalance principle with water admitted to, or let out of, tanks under the cars, so enabling the (heavier) descending one to pull the other up the 1 in 1.8 gradient by means of steel linking cables. Since 1944 the cars have been wound electrically, and have lost their water tanks (and attendants), as seen here. ('Cleveland' Series, R.M. & S. Ltd, Shrewsbury)

The upper terminus of the funicular is on Castle Walk. The black-and-white structure on the lower roof of the red-brick station building, to the left of the passenger car, is the original 2,000-gallon water tank used to power the railway. Although a tourist attraction in its own right, the line provides a vital link between Low Town and High Town for any townsfolk unwilling, or unable, to make the ascent on foot. (*Valentine's Series, posted 1919*)

A gate on the northern side of High Town has existed since the thirteenth century, standing above the old north moat of the town's defences. The present gate dates from 1740 and was built in brick but clad in stone in 1910 to commemorate Thomas Martin Southwell, founder of the carpet works in Low Town; it is the only survivor of five such gates in the town wall. The view is from the town's Market Place. (*L. Wilding, The Salop Art Press, Shrewsbury*)

By the twelfth century the Norman earl, Robert de Bellesmere, son of Roger de Montgomery, had built a castle in the town and it remained an important frontier fortress during the Normans' wars with Wales. In 1646, during the English Civil Wars, Parliamentary forces blew up the castle; the ruins of the toppled keep (left) now provide an attractive centrepiece to Tower Grounds park. The church of St Mary Magdalene, built by Telford on the site of a Norman church, is in the distance. (*Wilding & Son Ltd, Shrewsbury*)

Built in 1580 (and also damaged by the fire of 1646), this Tudor town house is famous for being the birthplace of the Revd Dr Thomas Percy (1729–1811), sometime Bishop of Dromore in County Down, periodical editor and general man of letters. Today he is perhaps best remembered for his *Reliques of English Poetry*, published in 1768, which prompted a revival of the ballad form in English poetry and helped start the whole English Romantic movement. (*Valentine's XL Series*)

The Severn Valley Railway station at Bridgnorth is seen here from Pan Pudding Hill. Opened in 1862, it was on the SVR's through route from Hartlebury, on the Oxford, Worcester & Wolverhampton Railway, to Shrewsbury. Both railways were eventually taken over by the GWR and passed to British Railways in 1948, with the SVR closing in 1963. The station survived and was reopened by the

BRIDGNORTH, FROM PAM PUDDING HILL

Severn Valley Railway Preservation Society on 23 May 1970 as the northern terminus of its steam railway to (since 1984) Kidderminster. Pan (also Pam) Pudding Hill is partly man-made, constructed as a siege emplacement by Henry I in 1101; in 1646 it was used as a gun battery for the bombardment of the town and castle. (*Jas. T. Foxall, Postern Gate, Bridgnorth*)

S 7033   CASTLE HILL, BRIDGNORTH

In 1895 Alfred Owen & Partners, for the local corporation, built a lattice-work footbridge with a 100yd span across Hollybush Road between the station and New Road so that travellers could pass between High Town and the station more easily. Seen here in about 1905, the bridge was allowed to decay after the railway closed in 1963, was itself closed as unsafe in 1970 and demolished four years later. Prompted by the success of the revived SVR and the resultant influx of visitors to the town, a trust was formed in 1994 to fund a new suspension footbridge, which was then built. (*Kingsway Real Photo Series*)

Bridgnorth is seen here from the south, with the High Town promontory overlooking the meadows forming the river's flood plain. As elsewhere around the country, in the past decade or so flood-plains have been seen as desirable building land and today this picture would show a modern housing development – still at risk of flooding and, perhaps worse, guilty of exacerbating such problems further downstream by allowing no release here for the swollen river. (*Valentine's Series*)

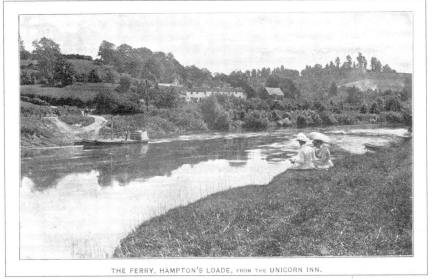

THE FERRY, HAMPTON'S LOADE, FROM THE UNICORN INN.

Hampton Loade is a small hamlet on the east bank of the Severn 5 miles from Bridgnorth. During the eighteenth and nineteenth centuries it was the site of an iron forge with a chain ferry, operated by the river current, being added in 1880 to link the hamlet with Hampton on the west bank where, in 1862, the SVR had opened a station (confusingly named Hampton Loade). This scene is little changed today on what is certainly the longest unspoilt stretch of the mature river: the iron industry has gone but the ferry still operates a seasonal service, and the Unicorn Inn can still be visited by railway passengers, walkers and cyclists for some much-needed refreshment. (*Unidentified, posted 1905*)

4

The Worcestershire Severn

The low hills and green meadows are always pleasant to
look upon; here and there weirs check the natural efforts
of the stream to increase its velocity, and it becomes
navigable for boats, barges and small steamers.
                                          (*The Severn Valley*, Great Western Railway, 2nd edn, 1923)

Beyond Bridgnorth the Severn Way continues to follow the west bank of
the river, sandwiched between the Severn and the SVR until Upper Arley
(109¾ miles) where it crosses to the opposite bank; thereafter it follows the
river closely through Worcestershire with only slight detours above and below
Worcester.

(*'JAYEMJAY' Series, Jackson & Son, Grimsby*)

Leaving Bridgnorth, the Severn crosses from Shropshire into Worcestershire, where the first riverside village encountered is Upper Arley. A ferry once operated from here, across to the SVR station on the western bank, and can just be made out left of centre in this view, between the two massed moorings of hire boats. (*Unidentified, posted 1905*)

Arley was once known as Ernley, roughly translated as 'an opening in the woods where eagles live'. St Peter's Church overlooks the ferry, whose service dated back to the twelfth century but sadly is no longer in use since replaced by a footbridge in 1972. (The carriage of vehicles had ceased in 1946.) The old ferryboat was taken downstream to Bewdley and moored at Severnside North; there she sank in a winter flood and after several years was broken up where she lay. (*Sepiatone Series, The Photochrom Co. Ltd, London and Tunbridge Wells, posted 1912*)

Here the Severn Way crosses to the eastern bank via the footbridge.

The preserved section of the SVR crosses the Severn just once, below Arley, on the Victoria Bridge. Cast in Coalbrookdale in 1862, it was designed by Sir John Fowler (1817–98), an eminent railway and bridge engineer of the mid-Victorian period. The bridge is a sister to the Albert Edward Bridge at Coalbrookdale featured earlier – and named after Victoria's son, the future King Edward VII. (*Unidentified, posted 1905*)

The Victoria Bridge from the west bank, looking upstream. The bank is a popular spot to observe trains crossing the bridge, which was featured in the 1978 remake of *The Thirty-Nine Steps*, starring Robert Powell, standing in for the Forth Bridge of Hitchcock's original 1935 masterpiece. Coincidentally, Fowler was joint engineer of the Scottish structure! (*E. Baylis & Son, Worcester, posted 1909*)

The bridge from slightly further downstream, looking from Seckley Wood on the north-eastern edge of the Wyre Forest across the river to Eymore Wood. (*The Wrench Series, posted 1905*)

The Severn Way is now sandwiched again between the SVR and the river, this time on the eastern bank.

The Severn above Bewdley has not been navigable for anything but the lightest of craft for many decades, though the idea is mooted periodically of making it so by the construction of weirs – a move firmly resisted by those who enjoy the tranquillity of this unspoilt stretch of the river. For a major river, it is remarkably shallow in places – especially during the summer – with a number of ancient fording points such as this one between Seckley Wood and Eymore Wood. To the right of this view today is Trimpley Reservoir, built in the 1960s to supplement Birmingham's water supply from the Elan Valley in mid-Wales and where boating is permitted. (*Unidentified*)

A picturesque view of the river upstream from Bewdley, where the shallowness of the water can be seen to better advantage. It is not always as peaceful as this, though: when in flood, the Severn is more than capable of covering both banks here. The river was declared 'a Navigation', or public right of way, by Act of Parliament in 1430, though since then the highest navigable point has migrated steadily downstream from Pool Quay. (*Valentine's Series*)

A similar view, with the obligatory cattle cooling themselves in the river – a scene that can be enjoyed today, either from the Severn Way or from a carriage on the SVR. (*The Wrench Series*)

A little south of Trimpley Reservoir is Bewdley Aqueduct, built to carry the water pipeline from the Elan Valley reservoirs in Wales, opened by King Edward VII in 1904, to supply the huge and growing needs of the city of Birmingham. For much of its west to east course across the country the pipeline is buried underground, though here and there it surfaces to cross rivers and railways. (*The Wrench Series*)

The next structure to cross the Severn, between Bewdley Aqueduct and the town, was Dowles Bridge. Built to take the Tenbury & Bewdley Railway over the river, it was opened to passengers in 1864; the railway was amalgamated with the GWR in 1869, nationalised in 1948 and then closed by BR in the early 1960s. The latticework of the bridge was dismantled in 1966 but the stone piers remain to fuel enthusiasts' dreams of – one day – a branch off the SVR, halfway up the hillside on the left, into the Wyre Forest. (*Sepiatone Series, The Photochrom Co. Ltd, London and Tunbridge Wells*)

The Falls, Wyre Forest, Bewdley.

Dowles Bridge took its name from the Dowles Brook which flows through the Wyre Forest and into the Severn immediately downstream of the old bridge. With the decline of navigation on this stretch a ford was made here as the river silted up. The Wyre Forest has long been a popular place for ramblers, cyclists and wildlife observers, the falls on the Dowles Brook being but one of its myriad attractions. (*E.P. Shepherd, Bewdley, V. & S. Ltd*)

Dowles Bridge again, looking towards Bewdley in the distance, with an arm of the Wyre Forest reaching down to the water's edge on the right. The name Bewdley is a corruption of the medieval French *beau lieu*, or 'beautiful place'. (*Unidentified*)

The earliest bridge at Bewdley, the next town on the Severn and a strategic crossing point on the river, was constructed in 1447, replacing a ford. This view, looking north, shows Thomas Telford's three-arched bridge built 1795–9 to link Bewdley on the west bank with the settlement of Wribbenhall on the east, beyond which lay the important manufacturing centres of Kidderminster, Stourbridge and Birmingham. The derelict Wribbenhall Quay is in the foreground, superseded by those on the opposite bank. At the highest floods the river can reach the very top of the bridge, which then has to be closed. (*Valentine's Series, posted 1907*)

> *Strictly speaking the Severn Way does not run through Bewdley,*
> *but through Wribbenhall (113½ miles).*

The quay on the west bank, above the bridge, known as Severnside North, still home to a Mug House pub. The scene is much changed today: the houses remain but the hire boats and the swimming baths hut have gone, and the roadway is now paved and railed off from the river with a movable flood defence wall in place – before it was installed in 2003–4, winter floods would frequently swamp the ground floors of the houses. (*Shepherd's Series, V. & S. Ltd, posted 1907*)

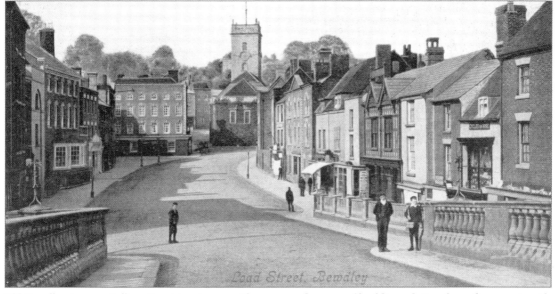

Old Bewdley is essentially a Georgian town, with a preponderance of buildings dating from the seventeenth and eighteenth centuries. It declined economically after the cutting of the Staffordshire & Worcester Canal in 1772, which connected the industrial heartland of the Black Country with Stourport downstream on the river, though the benefit of this was that the town's architecture remained relatively unscathed. Load Street, leading from the bridge in the foreground through Market Square to St Anne's Church, is the main thoroughfare, flanked by the Town Hall, Post Office, George Hotel and Angel Inn. (*Unidentified*)

Severnside South, Bewdley, from the east bank of the river. Like its counterpart north of the bridge, this was a busy quayside during the seventeenth and eighteenth centuries, exporting charcoal and coal from the Wyre Forest and wool from Wales; snuff making, rope spinning, bark peeling and tanning, brass founding and pewter making were locally developed industries. This townscape, like that of Load Street, is little changed today, although the quayside warehouses have now been converted into shops, offices and apartments protected by a second, new flood defence wall. (*Unidentified, posted 1904*)

Caves at Blackstone Rocks just below Bewdley (by the modern bypass bridge) once offered shelter to hermits, and to travellers waiting to cross when the river was too high. One legendary hermit was Sir Harry Wade, who moved in after his wife had been abducted (or had eloped) on his wedding day, and killed when Sir Harry fought with the other man. Wade gained a reputation as a holy man and one day, years later, a stranger came to him for penance for fighting over a knight's wife. Sir Harry revealed himself and grappled with the other man, only for both to plunge to their deaths in a whirlpool below. (*T.F.W. Harris, Bewdley*)

On the bank of the river opposite Blackstone Rocks lies the village of Ribbesford. As it had no cemetery, coffins had to be carried to St Anne's in Bewdley for burial along Ribbesford Lane (captioned here as Ribbesford Avenue), leading to the path being popularly known as 'the Coffin Way'. (*Unidentified, posted 1905*)

The wooded slopes of Stagborough Hill rise out of Ribbesford Woods less than a mile north-west of Stourport. Picturesque and unspoilt when this card was posted, today little in the landscape has changed. (*S. Hildersheimer & Co. Ltd, London and Manchester, posted 1909*)

THE SEVERN AT STOURPORT.

Stourport-on-Severn is unique among English towns in that it was built entirely as a result of the arrival of a canal. The famous canal engineer James Brindley (1716–72) can rightly be said to be the town's founder. Besides being a river and canal port, from the middle of the nineteenth century Stourport began to develop as a holiday town, popular with day trippers and holidaymakers from Birmingham and the Black Country arriving by the SVR from Hartlebury or Bewdley, or by electric tram from Kidderminster. This view is looking upstream from the bridge. (*H.L. Hodges, Kidderminster*)

Three bridges have stood at this point, the first of *c.* 1775 being that known as Brindley's Bridge, after the consulting engineer to the Staffordshire & Worcester Canal (and possibly built to his design), which was destroyed by floods in 1794; the second, built in 1806, was replaced in about 1870 by the present structure seen here by the pleasure steamers that plied their trade downstream between here, Holt Fleet and Worcester in the summer months – much as they do today. (*Sabrina Series, Haywood & Son, Stourport, posted 1915*)

The bridge and the east bank steamer moorings again; the white building on the west bank is the Stourport boathouse. A boat club was established here after the arrival of the canal, though the first Stourport Regatta was not held until 1892 – when the local club swept the board by winning every event! The club is still going strong, its members training and competing in events throughout the year. (*Valentine's Series*)

Looking upstream from the bridge – where the tramway from Kidderminster terminated – with more steamers, and floating swimming baths (opened 1879), moored on the east bank to tempt visitors with their pleasures. After the canal arrived, river trade above this point declined and this became about the most northerly navigable point on the Severn, with the reaches beyond silting up and reclaimed by vegetation to become a favourite abode of walkers and fishermen. (*Valentine's Series*)

River steamers head downstream from Stourport. The sandstone cliff is Redstone Rock which, like Blackstone Rocks higher up, is riddled with caves and hewn-out shelters once serving as hermitages, refuges for travellers, and hideouts for bandits. Originally this reach of the river was tidal and, until locks and weirs downstream raised the height of the river, it was one of the best crossing points at low tide between Bewdley and Worcester and as such used by the funeral cortège of Prince Arthur (1486–1502), son of Henry VII, on its way from Ludlow Castle to Worcester Cathedral. A nearby ferry, originally worked by monks from at least the thirteenth century, was being operated by the cave-dwelling Glover family when the last Stourport Bridge opened, after which they were compensated for loss of livelihood. (*Unidentified*)

Lincomb Lock, below Redstone Rock, was built on the site of Cloth House Ford, which connected a route from Titton on the east bank to small settlements at Larford and Astley (now a suburb of Stourport) on the other. It was built in 1844 on dry land on the east bank, then a channel cut to it, so forming a new island in the river. Cloth House Ford derives its name from the cloth fulling mills on Titton Brook while the lock takes its name from the nearby village of Lincomb a little to the south. (*Valentine's Series*)

Above Lincomb Lock is Lincomb Weir, built at the same time to raise the river level in the new channel. Here the shallower waters below the weir attract children with their boat, as well as cattle. (*W. Cane, Stourport, posted 1918*)

Before the construction of Lincomb Lock many hazards to navigation existed on the river from Worcester up to Stourport arising from tidal variations and low water levels during dry periods; boats therefore had often to be manhandled by teams of bow-haulicrs when sailing conditions were unsuitable. The lock, seen here from the south, is 100ft long and 20ft wide with a drop of 7ft; the footbridge on the right crosses Titton Brook at its confluence with the Severn. (*W.T. Hodges, Kidderminster, posted 1908*)

Below Lincomb
Lock is the
village of Holt
Fleet, 6 miles
from Stourport,
where there is
also another
weir and lock to
help maintain
water levels so
as to keep the
river navigable.
(*Unidentified*)

*The Severn Way crosses to the west bank of the river via the bridge shown in the top picture
of this multi-view card, thereafter making a slight detour away from the river.*

The minor road between Holt Fleet Lock and Holt Fleet Bridge is still in use today, and also serves holiday chalets along the riverbank. (*Boots Cash Chemists 'Pelham' Series*)

As at Lincomb, an island has been formed at Holt Fleet with the lock in its own channel separate from the main body of the river. Like its counterpart, the lock is 100ft long and 20ft wide and was excavated in 1844. The view here is from Holt Heath, on the west bank of the Severn, looking downstream. (*W*)

Steamer Anchored, Holt Fleet.

A second, multi-view card of three more scenes at Holt Fleet. Again, the publisher is not known but was very probably from the area, such cards being sold as souvenirs in local shops and places of refreshment. These cards were popular purchases as the buyer obtained a number of views for the price of one! (*Unidentified*)

The Cafe from River, Holt Fleet.

The Weir, Holt Fleet.

Holt Fleet Bridge was designed and built by Thomas Telford, and dates from 1828. He was also responsible for six other bridges spanning the Severn: at Montford, Buildwas, Bridgnorth, Bewdley, Tewkesbury and Gloucester, all constructed during the period from the early 1790s to the early 1830s. (*Valentine's Series, posted 1906*)

The weir at Holt Fleet, a popular spot for picnickers during the latter years of the nineteenth century and the first years of the twentieth. Part of the message on this card reads: 'We are having a nice time. Went to see this place this morning. It is a lovely place.' (*Frith's Series, F. Frith & Co. Ltd, Reigate, posted c. 1914*)

The Holt Fleet Hotel catered for the many visitors who arrived by steamer, charabanc or even bicycle. The large wooden building next to the hotel, alongside the river, was used for dining and as a tea-room. The original inn was demolished in the 1930s and a new one built. (*Henry Wood, Birmingham*)

An unidentified river steamer passes the hotel and landing stage at Holt Fleet. The spot was a very popular destination for river trips from both Stourport and Worcester, and during summer weekends and on bank holidays the steamers would be packed. (*Frith's Series, F. Frith & Co. Ltd, Reigate*)

Edwardian visitors to Holt Fleet enjoyed this attractive view from the bridge. The tranquil charm of the riverside, woodlands, hills and lanes made for an ideal location for day trippers; it seemed a million miles from the smoke, grime and grind of Birmingham and the Black Country. (*Henry Wood, Birmingham, posted 1907*)

After its detour below Holt Fleet, the Severn Way heads south through Holt and rejoins the river east of the village of Grimley, about a mile above the Camp House Inn (126¾ miles).

The Camp House Inn above Worcester, formerly a watermen's inn (licensed by Oliver Cromwell after the Battle of Worcester in 1651) and the site of a punt ferry; until Bevere (or Camp) Lock and Weir were built there in 1846 by Bevere (Camp) Island there was a bar across the Severn, which occasioned great delays to traffic when the river was low. A beauty spot frequented by summer strollers from the city, the inn takes its name from the island's rather less happy use as a camp by the citizens of Worcester fleeing the city to escape the ravages of war or – for the last time in 1637 – the plague. Happily, pints are still pulled and food served, the inn preserving an old-world charm that welcomes guests today as surely as it did when this souvenir was purchased a century ago. (*Ebenezer Baylis & Son, Worcester*)

The Worcester coat of arms is displayed on this card, along with two scenes from the river immediately north of the city. The motto reads: *Civitas in bello in pace fidelis* (In war, in peace, a faithful city) – a reference to its long-standing loyalty to the Crown. (*Unidentified, posted 1905*)

The now-vanished Kepax Ferry once crossed the river north of Pitchcroft Racecourse on the edge of Worcester, serving the residential area of Barbourne on the east bank; it was popular with Victorian and Edwardian walkers who would visit the water meadows around Hallow and the Camp House Inn on the opposite side before returning via Camp House Ferry, now also long gone. (*Exclusive Celesque Series, The Photochrom Co. Ltd, London and Tunbridge Wells*)

Another river steamer full of trippers from Worcester heads past Kepax Ferry for a day out at Holt Fleet or Stourport. Many of them would have purchased a circular tour ticket that permitted travel one way on the steamer and return either by road or rail – the GWR issued such tickets from its stations' booking offices. (*Frith's Series, F. Frith & Co. Ltd, Reigate*)

Below the Kepax Ferry was another one at the Dog and Duck Inn. The name marked the inn as a venue for a particularly cruel blood sport favoured on the Severn: punters would bet on which dog from a pack would be the first to catch and kill a duck in the river; so that the duck did not fly off, its wings were clipped before being released. By the middle of the nineteenth century the 'sport' had thankfully disappeared and the inn was later converted into a house for the ferryman. (*Frith's Series, F. Frith & Co. Ltd, Reigate, posted 1912*)

The Dog and Duck Ferry again, with the city's suburbs encroaching noticeably. A young man is taking his lady for a gentle row on the river – perhaps in a skiff hired from the cabin at the moorings on the right. (*Unidentified, posted 1903*)

C.45862. WORCESTER: GRAND STAND & BOAT.

The racecourse at Pitchcroft, immediately beside the river on its eastern bank, dates back to the eighteenth century. The Grand Stand Hotel seen here no longer exists, but the racing flourishes. The river steamer is heading up towards Bevere Lock. In 1992 a footbridge – Sabrina Bridge – was opened here to provide an alternative river crossing to the extremely busy road bridge below it. (*Celesque Series, The Photochrom Co. Ltd, London and Tunbridge Wells*)

Sabrina Bridge is used by the Severn Way to take walkers over to the east bank.

Worcester's commercial river traffic, and pleasure steamers, berthed primarily at South Quay and North Quay on the eastern bank of the river. This is looking to part of North Quay (above the bridge), served by a branch of the GWR from Worcester Foregate Street station – note the solitary wagon behind the steamer and the tunnel through the bridge taking the line on to South Quay. (*Valentine's Series*)

The Severn Bridge at Worcester, also known as the Worcester Bridge, was designed by John Gwynn (sometimes spelled Gwyn or Gwynne), architect of the English Bridge at Shrewsbury and Atcham Bridge, and was completed in 1781. Before construction the cost of bridge, land, quay walls and approaches was estimated at £5,230 but in the event totalled nearly £30,000! Here two pleasure steamers – note the upper-deck seats on one – lie at the quay beside Hylton Road on the west bank. (*W*)

In 1847 the carriageway on the bridge was widened from 24ft to 32ft, then in 1931–2 the whole structure was substantially rebuilt, severing the quayside tramway in order to accommodate an increase in motor traffic, though traffic on the day this photograph was taken is distinctly absent. It was officially opened by the Prince of Wales the following year. (*Valentine's Series, posted 1934*)

The latest in a long line of structures stretching back to at least the eleventh century, this is the new (and current) bridge as seen from the south, looking across to the quayside warehouses – now apartments and restaurants. The postcard sender has written: 'We walked over this bridge last night – have had a nice run here, and a comfortable night at the Crown Hotel.' ('*Phototype' Postcard, Valentine & Sons Ltd, Dundee and London, posted 1952*)

The Severn in Worcester, looking northwards from the cathedral tower, with the edge of the County Cricket Ground, off New Road, on the very left of the card. Only from such a high vantage point can the sheer scale of the railway's crossing of the river, by the racecourse, be fully appreciated; opened in 1860 (and rebuilt in 1904) the viaduct still carries the former GWR route to Malvern and Hereford. (*The Photochrom Co. Ltd, Tunbridge Wells*)

One of Worcester's electric trams heads towards The Cross, in the centre of the city, on Broad Street, having just crossed the river and climbed Bridge Street; today road traffic is limited to pedestrians using Crowngate Shopping Centre, the open-air market and the still-plentiful shops. (*Valentine's Series, posted 1908*)

The Cross is the name given to the intersection of Foregate Street, St Swithin's Street, High Street and Broad Street, though the actual stone cross that once stood here is long gone. The tram here is heading north, towards Foregate Street. (*Valentine's Series, posted 1905*)

A little way east of The Cross stands King Charles's House, one of the city's old buildings made famous by the Civil War, and now a shop. Here Charles II stayed during the Battle of Worcester and from which he narrowly escaped when Roundhead soldiers broke in at the front door. (*Frith's Series, F. Frith & Co. Ltd, Reigate*)

Continuing along Foregate Street, the road passes under the bridge carrying the former GWR's Worcester Foregate Street station, opened in 1860, to the left of which is the long viaduct taking the railway over the Severn. Apart from the shops' signs and contents, the scene is little changed today. (*Valentine's Series, posted 1907*)

Shire Hall and Victoria Institute, Worcester.

The horse-cab rank and shelter are no longer there, a bus and cycle lane has replaced the tram track, and there are substantially more cars than bicycles, but otherwise this view of the Shire Hall and the Victoria Institute just north of the Foregate Street bridge is much the same today; the latter building was erected in the 1890s as a memorial of Queen Victoria's Golden Jubilee and houses the city's public library, art gallery and museum. The lady cyclist appears to have anticipated the route of the cycle lane by a century or so, running as it does in her direction against the one-way flow of motor traffic. (*Unidentified, posted 1905*)

Worcester High Street extends south from The Cross, in the opposite direction to that taken by Foregate Street, its trams serving the affluent southern housing suburbs along the London and Bath roads until the system closed in 1928.
(*The Star Series, O.D. & D.L.*)

Another view of the High Street, this time looking north towards The Cross. The improvements of the postcard caption refer to the 1903–4 conversion of the city's horse tramways to electric traction, known locally as 'the Worcester Tramway Siege' because of the disruption and inconvenience the work caused. (*Harvey Barton's Series*)

Worcester Guildhall on the High Street, built in 1721–4, was designed by Thomas White, though the council chamber and assembly room only date from 1791, when George Byfield redesigned it. Sir Gilbert Scott and the City Architect Henry Rowe refurbished the building again in the 1870s. A devil's head, nailed by its ears above the doorway, is said to represent Oliver Cromwell. (*Frith's Series, F. Frith & Co. Ltd, Reigate*)

Another of Worcester's old buildings of note is the Commandery, at the junction of the Bath and London roads. The site was originally occupied by a hospital founded by St Wulfstan, Bishop of Worcester from 1062 to 1095; the present building dates from the 1460s and achieved fame during the Civil Wars as the headquarters of the future King Charles II's Royalist forces during the unsuccessful 1651 defence of Worcester. It is now a museum. (*The Commandery Series, Joseph Littlebury, The Commandery, Worcester*)

Between the Commandery and the river is the cathedral, approached from the landward side through the fourteenth-century Edgar Tower. It was once the entrance to the Norman castle (the other remains of which have long since been demolished, stolen and levelled) and was restored to its present state in the nineteenth century. (*Frith's Series, F. Frith & Co. Ltd, Reigate*)

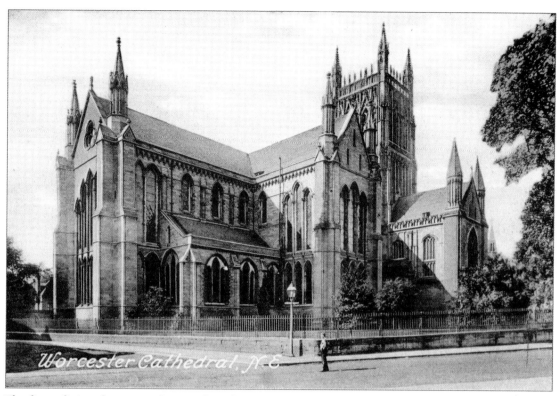

The first religious house on this site dates back to at least AD 680 and was almost certainly a wooden structure; the present building was begun, in stone, in 1084 by Bishop Wulfstan – the only Saxon bishop allowed by the Norman conquerors to retain his see – with substantial work being carried out between 1225 and 1395; refurbishment was undertaken between 1859 and 1874 under Sir Gilbert Scott. (*Frith's Series, F. Frith & Co. Ltd, Reigate*)

The fourteenth-century cloisters exit into the cathedral grounds on the east bank of the Severn below the road bridge. Worcester was the lowest fording point on the river in post-Roman times; hence its importance as a military, commercial and consequently religious settlement. (*Frith's Series, F. Frith & Co. Ltd, Reigate*)

WORCESTER CATHEDRAL FROM THE RIVER WALK   13575

Worcester Cathedral from across the Severn, with the riverside walk in the foreground running alongside the Worcestershire County Cricket Club's ground and adjoining playing fields. (*Salmon Series, J. Salmon Ltd, Sevenoaks*)

The cathedral from a little further downstream – a favourite vantage point of artists and photographers wishing to capture its best aspect. Proposals were once made to extend the South Quay tramway past the cathedral to Diglis Locks downriver, but had to be abandoned when the clergy raised objections. Cathedral, or Priory, Ferry operated from the steps in the embankment on the right. (*Valentine's Series*)

The cathedral, painted by Arthur C. Payne from the same vantage point, shows a typical shallow-draught Severn trow passing by. Once a familiar sight on the river, their use declined with the coming of the railways as commercial traffic withered away and by the golden age of the postcard at the beginning of the twentieth century they had all but vanished. (*S. Hildersheimer & Co. Ltd, London and Manchester, posted 1906*)

Cathedral Ferry, seen here leaving the steps, is crossing to Chapter Meadows and what is now the County Cricket Club's ground. The ferry was established by monks from the cathedral priory – hence its other name – and was certainly in use by the time the Watergate, centre, was built in the latter part of the fourteenth century. Presumably this card was bought as a souvenir, for it was posted in The Netherlands to an address in Leiden. (*Frith's Series, F. Frith & Co. Ltd, Reigate, posted 1903*)

The South Quay, with a pleasure steamer awaiting passengers alongside one derelict and one sunken hulk used as mooring pontoons. The riverside walk is little changed today, though railings have been put along the edge – and the swans are more numerous than ever. (*RA Series, R.A. (Postcards) Ltd, London*)

WORCESTER CATHEDRAL from the BRIDGE. 19.

92 VIEW FROM DEANERY GARDENS, WORCESTER.

Looking back, from the riverside entrance to the cathedral by way of the deanery gardens, to the South Quay. The elegant spire – a long-time city landmark known as 'the Glover's Needle' – is all that remains of St Andrew's Church; 245ft in height, its width tapers from 20ft at its base on the tower to less than 7in at its apex. (*Kingsway Real Photo Series, WHS, posted 1911*)

This promenade, Diglis Parade, continues the Severn Way southwards to Diglis Locks (131 miles).

Worcester. From the Weir   Fine Art & Photographic Depot, Worcester

The third and final weir/lock set downriver from Stourport was built here, at Diglis, in 1844 after the Worcester & Birmingham Canal Co. had opened its canal into the Severn in 1815, this becoming the main trade route linking the river with the Midlands. Today the commercial barges have gone, their place taken by private and hired narrowboats, and other small craft. A mile below Diglis Basins, where the canal joins the river, the River Teme enters the Severn at the site of the 1651 Battle of Worcester. (*Fine Art & Photographic Depot, Worcester, posted 1904*)

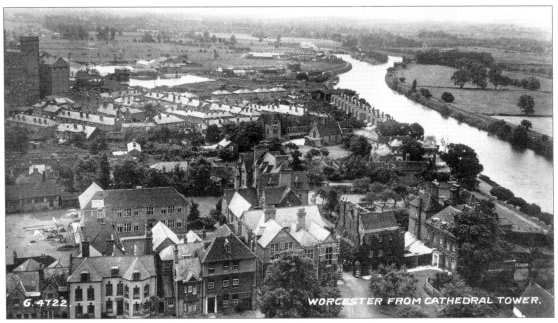

G.4722   WORCESTER FROM CATHEDRAL TOWER.

The river from the tower of the cathedral again, this time looking downstream towards the canal basins (left), and weir and locks by the island (right) at Diglis. The terrace of small houses on the riverbank, like the cricket ground, is just as prone to flooding now as then; most years see all the open fields here covered in water. The blocks of terraces in the centre are houses built for the workers in the Royal Worcester Porcelain Works, off the card to the left. (*Valentine's Series*)

RUINS OF THE GUESTEN HALL, WORCESTER.

A final look at Worcester: the ruins of Guesten Hall, in the grounds of the cathedral. This fourteenth-century priory building once provided hospitality to guests but was allowed to fall into disrepair as a picturesque ruin. The roof, however, has been saved and erected as part of a new Guesten Hall, a venue for exhibitions, concerts and other public events at the Avoncroft Museum of Buildings near Bromsgrove. (*Unidentified*)

Downstream from Worcester the Severn enters an ever-widening flood plain, overlooked from the west by the 8-mile range of the Malvern Hills; Ivy Scar Rock protrudes from the side of the most northerly of them, the prosaically named North Hill, the summit of which is 1,305ft above sea level. (*Valentine's 'Photo Brown' Postcards*)

MALVERN & IVY SCAR ROCK

Opposite the Malverns, the Severn Way makes the last of its Worcestershire detours to take a 2-mile short-cut across a loop in the river.

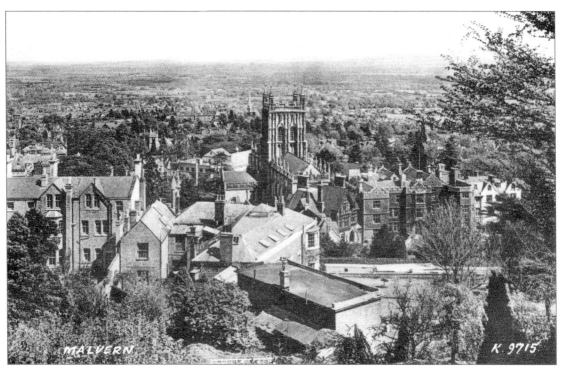

The town of Great Malvern nestles into the lower slopes of the Malverns above the Severn plain. The priory, centre, stands on ground about 200ft above sea level while the flat expanse of the valley floor is just 50ft high. (*'Sepiatype' Postcard, Valentine & Son, Dundee and London*)

A dramatic view of the extensive Severn plain is provided here, framed by Wyche Cutting just south of the Worcestershire Beacon summit in the Malvern range. The view is to the south-east, in the direction of Upton upon Severn. The Wyche was an ancient pass over the hills on the route of a saltway from Rhydd on the Severn into Herefordshire; the cutting was dug in 1840 and takes the B4218 road to Colwall. (*Frith's Series, posted 1904*)

THE SEVERN VALLEY FROM THE WYCHE. GT. MALVERN.

The Severn Plain from a similar but slightly lower vantage point, with the valley floor apparently receding into the infinite distance beyond the First World War-era army camp. Entering the picture halfway up on the left and gradually curving away above the camp is the former railway branch line from Great Malvern to Upton and Tewkesbury, now obliterated by farming and, on the sweep of its bend, the Three Counties Showground. (*Unidentified*)

84662   Upton-on-Severn from River   Frith's

The charming little town of Upton upon Severn lies some 6 miles south of Worcester, and like that city is prone to flooding when the river rises, being built on low-lying ground on the west bank. Indeed, it is not uncommon some winters to see all the riverside fields between the two places under water. The 'Pepperpot' in the distance is a 1769 copper cupola atop the surviving thirteenth-century tower of a church demolished in the 1930s. (*Frith's Series*)

The High Street, Upton-on-Severn (the precise form of the name has varied over the years), probably in the mid-1930s to judge by the motor cars. The town is about 6 miles north of Tewkesbury, with the Worcestershire–Gloucestershire boundary crossing the Severn roughly midway between the two. (*RA Series, R.A. (Postcards) Ltd, London*)

The 1930s bridge at Upton, which carries the A4104 to the village of Ryall on the east bank, before continuing on over the M5 to Pershore on the other side of the Severn Plain. An important port in the Middle Ages, the town now relies on agriculture and tourism for its economic prosperity. The bridge is the latest in a series beginning in the fifteenth century, and is the only one across the river between Worcester and Tewkesbury. (*RA Series, R.A. (Postcards) Ltd, London*)

The bridge is taken by the Severn Way as it crosses to the west bank (143 miles),
which it then follows all the way to Tewkesbury.

5

The Tidal River

There twice a day the Severn fills;
The salt sea-water passes by,
And hushes half the babbling Wye,
And makes a silence in the hills.
(Alfred, Lord Tennyson, *In Memoriam A.H.H.*, 1850)

At Tewkesbury (150 miles) the Severn Way makes a short detour up the Old
Avon, then back down the Mill Avon before rejoining the Severn to follow
closely its eastern bank all the way to Severn Beach (210½ miles), leaving the
river only at Slimbridge, where it passes on the landward side of the Wildfowl
& Wetlands Trust site there, Sharpness (the docks) and Berkeley (the power
station). For those wishing to continue on from Severn Beach, a 14½-mile trail
known as the Bristol Link takes walkers along the bank as far as Avonmouth,
and then beside the Somerset Avon into the heart of Bristol.

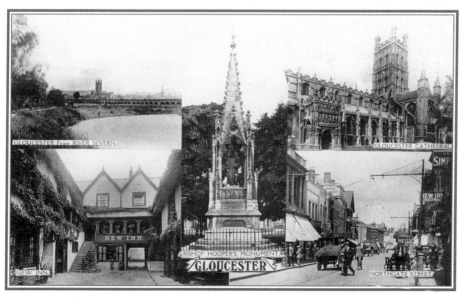

(*W&K, posted 1923*)

The Mythe Bridge at Tewkesbury. This elegant, single iron span was designed by Thomas Telford and constructed 1823–6; it carries what is now the A438 Ledbury road across the Severn just north of the town. The total length of the bridge is 276ft, with the cast-iron arch 170ft long. It was reinforced in 1923 when a concrete slab was laid over the original iron decking. (*Unidentified*)

The Mythe Bridge takes the Severn Way back to the east bank of the river.

At Tewkesbury the Warwickshire Avon meets the Severn after dividing into two channels: the Old Avon, which joins the Severn at Upper Lode, and the Mill Avon, which flows under King John's Bridge and joins the Severn at Lower Lode – lode, or loade, as a place-name derives from the Anglo-Saxon word for ford. (*Valentine's Series*)

Tewkesbury Cross is at the junction of Church Street, Barton Street and the High Street, where the town's first market was held. This view, looking north towards King John's Bridge, is little changed today – there are over two hundred listed buildings in the town and in 1967 its centre was designated a conservation area. (*Tewkesbury Register & Gazette*)

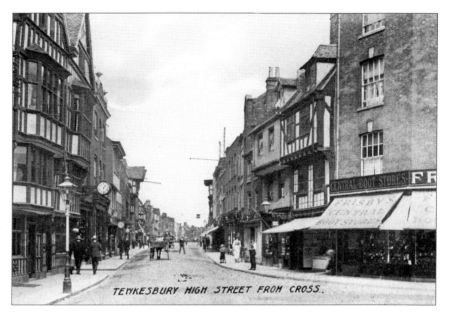

Robert FitzHamon, a kinsman of William the Conqueror, founded the Benedictine abbey of Tewkesbury shortly after the Norman Conquest, with much of the stone for its construction brought by sea from Normandy. Remarkably, its church (dating from 1090) escaped the Dissolution of the Monasteries when the townsfolk bought it from King Henry VIII for £453 – the value of the lead on the roof and the metal in the bells! The church boasts the largest central Norman tower in the world which, 46ft square, rises to a height of 132ft. (*Unidentified*)

Dating back to the fifteenth century and once a coaching inn, the (Royal) Hop Pole Hotel is now an AA 3-star hotel with a rear garden leading to the Mill Avon; the arms of Queen Mary, a visitor to the inn, are displayed on the portico above the Church Street entrance. The hotel was mentioned by Charles Dickens in *The Pickwick Papers* (1837): 'At the Hop Pole at Tewkesbury they stopped to dine; upon which occasion there was more bottled ale, with some more Madeira, and some Port besides.' (*Raphael Tuck & Sons*)

Advertisement from the pre-First World War '*Borough*' *Guide* to Tewkesbury.

Lower Lode was an ancient ferry crossing of the Severn just below Tewkesbury, close to where the river is joined by the Mill Avon; this view is from the western, or Forthampton, bank of the Severn. The name suggests that there was once a ford here, replaced by the ferry in medieval times as the river was made more navigable through natural and human intervention. (*The Star Series, G.D. & D., London*)

The fifteenth-century Lower Lode Inn is on the east bank near the village of Forthampton, its riverside frontage today little changed in the hundred years or so since this card was published. Now a hotel and restaurant, it also offers a site for touring caravans and moorings for leisure craft – and a ferry service. (*G.E.P.W. Series, Tewkesbury*)

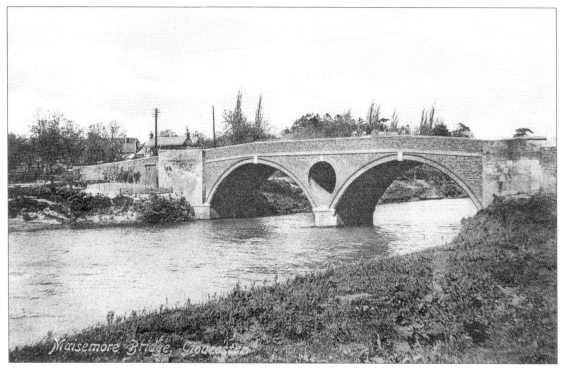

The Severn divides just above Gloucester, at Upper Parting near Maisemore, to enclose Alney Island and, by so doing, provided in the past a natural double-ditch line of defence on the western side of the city. (The name Maisemore probably derives from the Welsh *maes mawr* or 'great field'.) This stone bridge, over the western arm of the river, was built in the eighteenth century to replace an earlier structure; it was replaced in turn in 1956. The large opening between the two arches was to help let flood water through. (*Frith's Series, F. Frith & Co., Reigate*)

This is the East Channel of the Severn as it approaches Gloucester; Archdeacon Meadow lies to the left of the riverside path. St Catherine's Viaduct, seen in front of the city and cathedral, carries the GWR South Wales main line to Black Bridge swing bridge over the East Channel. Part of the message on the card reads 'The college work I find awfully hard, and on Friday collapsed under it had to lie down for 2 hrs but now am quite alright again.' (*Valentine's Series, posted 1911*)

The Severn Way follows the eastern arm of the river through Gloucester (161 miles).

After the railway bridge comes Westgate Bridge, the view from it here showing the river steamer *River Queen* approaching. The hire boats on the right are moored alongside a water meadow while on the left are Alney Terrace and West End Parade. There have been four incarnations of Westgate Bridge: the original twelfth-century structure was replaced in 1809, 1974 and 1999. Well before the first bridge was built a settlement – Glevum – was founded here by the Romans, this being the lowest safe fording place on the Severn at that period and hence of great strategic importance. (*C.J. Goddard, Gloucester*)

The Midland Railway boasted the quickest and most direct route between Birmingham and Cheltenham, Gloucester, Bath, Bristol and the West of England; here a Johnson 2–4–0 express locomotive departs with its train from the MR's busy Gloucester station on one of these services. (*The Alphalsa Publishing Co. Ltd, London*)

From as early as the seventh century a church stood on the site of the present cathedral; a Benedictine monastery dedicated to St Peter was established in 1022 and the building of today's structure was begun in 1089 by the Norman Abbot Serlo of Bayeux. In 1540 the monastery was dissolved but the church was rededicated the following year, to the Holy Trinity, as a cathedral. (*Frith's Series, F. Frith & Co. Ltd, Reigate*)

The building of the cathedral nave was started towards the end of the eleventh century, though a disastrous fire in 1122 delayed its completion until 1160; the blackening of the bases of some of the columns is said to be a visible legacy of the conflagration. The message on the card is simply 'Best Wishes for a Happy Xmas' – the use of postcards to convey such greetings being a common practice at the time. (*Unidentified, posted 1905*)

Looking down Eastgate Street from The Cross, where Northgate, Southgate, Eastgate and Westgate Streets all meet. Today, as a sign of the times, two shopping precincts now flank the street. (*The Photochrom Co. Ltd, London and Tunbridge Wells*)

In 1780, in this building on the corner of Park Street and St Catherine Street, one of the very first Sunday Schools was held, the brainchild of the newspaper publisher Robert Raikes. From it grew a whole nationwide movement. (*Celesque Series, The Photochrom Co. Ltd, London and Tunbridge Wells, posted 1919*)

The house in Southgate Street from where Raikes (1735–1811) published the *Gloucester Journal*. (*Celesque Series, The Photochrom Co. Ltd, London and Tunbridge Wells, posted 1916*)

The second Bishop of Gloucester, John Hooper (1495–1555), spent his last night in this house (centre left), in Westgate Street, in February 1555; the following day he was taken to St Mary's Square in front of the cathedral and burnt alive – though only after the third attempt at lighting the damp wood. His crime? Originally a Roman Catholic, he had embraced the Protestant faith and, when ordered to by Queen Mary Tudor, refused to recant. It is now the Gloucester Folk Museum. (*Excel Series*)

The New Inn on Northgate Street. Its name dates from its construction in about 1450 as accommodation for pilgrims visiting the tomb of King Edward II (1284–1327) in the cathedral, where miracles were reputed to occur – something perhaps not unconnected with the fact that such visitors provided an important source of income for the city. (*Unidentified, posted 1903*)

The Docks, Gloucester   Valentines Series   19792

With the opening of the Gloucester & Sharpness Canal in 1827, bypassing a treacherous downstream stretch of the Severn, sea-going vessels gained easier access to Gloucester, so encouraging the construction of a large docks complex. Here, looking north along the 1830s Baker's Quay, vessels are moored next to the Pillar & Lucy Warehouse while the brig on the left is berthed against Llanthony Quay, built 20 years later for coal exports brought in by rail from the Forest of Dean. Beyond is the Great Western Warehouse, burnt down in 1945, with the Alexandra Warehouse behind it. With the near-extinction of commercial waterborne traffic, regeneration over the last two decades has seen the warehouses put to new uses, including offices, restaurants, an antiques centre and – appropriately – the National Waterways Museum. (*Valentine's Series*)

Steamer Trips.

Steamers run up to Apperley (9 miles) on the Severn twice a day, generally about 10 a.m. and 3 p.m. during the summer months at a very small fare, starting from Westgate Bridge.

There is also a service of passenger ship boats running between Gloucester and Sharpness, on the canal, and one may take this voyage in summer, a couple of hours or so sufficing to traverse the length of the canal.

Boating.

For those who are fond of rowing there is an excellent opportunity at Gloucester, for there is the great waterway of the Severn all the way to Worcester, nearly 30 miles by river, and the Ship Canal to Sharpness, where, if the scenery is less inviting, at any rate there is no current.

There is always a good assortment of boats—outriggers, skiffs, punts, etc.—from which to choose at Westgate Bridge, where the boat builders and proprietors locate themselves.

Advice for those wishing to enjoy themselves by 'messing about in boats' on the river, from the pre-First World War *'Borough' Guide* to Gloucester.

The natural phenomenon known as the Severn Bore is generated in the estuary as a surge current caused by a particular combination of wind and tide at different times of the month, and takes the form of a series of four or five waves flowing upriver together at speeds of up to 13mph; the most spectacular waves – up to 10ft high – occur during the spring and autumn equinoxes and coincide with the highest tides. (*Frith's Series, F. Frith & Co. Ltd, Reigate*)

Postcard photographers chose popular viewpoints to capture the bore where it could be seen to best advantage as it roared round tight, shallower bends in the river, as here at Lower Parting where the two channels of the river combine again below Gloucester; this particular occasion has been precisely captioned as 4 September 1921. A follow-up phenomenon often missed by observers is 'the big muddy', so called because when the bore has passed, the river flows in the wrong direction for up to an hour, stops and stands still before the normal seaward flow returns. (*Unidentified*)

Now entering its old age, the Severn begins to wind this way and that in ever more exaggerated loops across its flat flood-plain. Close by, on slightly higher ground on its western bank some 8 miles from Gloucester, is the village of Westbury-on-Severn. (*Lilywhite Ltd, Brighouse*)

At Westbury the river makes a 180-degree bend; here, on the outside of the bend, can be seen the classic associated features of erosion (the cliffs in the background) and deposition (the sand in the foreground). Extreme right is the tip of the Arlingham peninsula, around which the river loops. The sender has written: 'Sorry we hadn't found this spot when you were down – it's just grand, 3 miles from our own front door – a lovely beach. We must show you when you come down in the autumn.' (*Unidentified, posted 1948*)

Two miles further on from Westbury-on-Severn lies Newnham. This view, from the hills above the village, takes in another great S-bend in the river with the southern edge of the Arlingham peninsula on the left and the Severn widening rapidly as it passes the Wildfowl & Wetlands Trust at Slimbridge, founded in 1946 by the naturalist Peter Scott, on the far bank, right. (*Unidentified*)

The Severn Way adheres faithfully to the shoreline all the way round the Arlingham peninsula, then makes a slight detour inland to follow the Gloucester & Sharpness Canal behind Slimbridge (183 miles).

Sailing boats on the Severn near Newnham – possibly being used for recreation or for fishing. Again, the features of a shifting river course are apparent; this, coupled with the presence of numerous sandbanks along this tidal stretch, led to the cutting of the 16-mile Gloucester & Sharpness Canal on the east bank to aid navigation. At the time of its construction it was the longest and deepest ship canal in the world. (*Tilley and Son, Ledbury, posted 1947*)

The old ferry to Arlingham at Newnham, at the point known as the Nab, with other commercial craft much in evidence; the large ferry boat could transport livestock and even carts. This reach of the river has always been noted for its fishing, especially elvers (young eels), and that royal delicacy of old, lampreys. (*Unidentified; photo credited to F. Blanton*)

Newnham again, this time at Newnham Pill, where the Whetstone Brook enters the river; a craft transports an unfeasibly large load of foliage of some kind. The card is a very early example, and almost certainly published locally: any message would have to be written below the picture, with the other side reserved for the address and stamp. (*Unidentified*)

Severn Bridge and Forest of Dean

This particular Severn Bridge was part of a railway route between the MR's Gloucester to Bristol line and the GWR's South Wales main line; it also served the Severn & Wye Railway in the Forest of Dean to the west of the river. Construction began in 1875, with the finished structure opening to passenger traffic on 21 July 1879. Although built where the river narrows briefly, with approaches it was 4,162ft long; clearance above high-water level was 70ft. The main channel of the river was bridged by two 327ft spans (far left), flanked by nineteen lesser spans and, here on the extreme right in front of its control cabin, a swing bridge to permit the passage of tall-rigged vessels. It also carried a gas main. (*The Cotswold Publishing Co. Ltd, Wotton-under-Edge*)

The Severn Bridge from the opposite, Forest of Dean, bank; in the foreground is Severn Bridge station. After the opening of the Severn Tunnel in 1886 (see p. 127) the fortunes of the operating company, the Severn & Wye & Severn Bridge Joint Railway, went into decline and 8 years later the concern was bought by the MR and GWR jointly and the bridge used as a relief route for the tunnel. In 1960, then in British Railways' ownership, it was badly damaged when hit by two tankers and the gas main exploded, welding the ships together; their wrecks can still be seen. It never reopened and five years later was demolished. (*Celesque Series, The Photochrom Co. Ltd, London and Tunbridge Wells*)

Immediately downstream from the site of the railway bridge, on the edge of the Forest of Dean opposite the mouth of the Gloucester & Sharpness Canal, is the town of Lydney with its once-prosperous small harbour, now a marina. The lock gates mark the entrance to a 1-mile canal linking the town, formerly on the river, to the Severn. On the Gloucester–South Wales railway line, the town is also home to the southern terminus of the Dean Forest Railway preserved steam line. (*Frith's Series*)

This view is looking west from Stinchcombe Hill, east of the Severn. Stinchcombe village lies at the foot of the hill, in the distance is the village of Berkeley – now home to a decommissioned nuclear power station – and beyond that, on the opposite bank, Lydney and the Forest of Dean. From the same vantage point today this rural panorama is bisected by the M5 motorway, which runs across the middle of the landscape just the other side of Stinchcombe. (*The Cotswold Publishing Co. Ltd, Wotton-under-Edge*)

GWR 'Star' Class 4–6–0 express locomotive 4002 *Evening Star* blasts its way out of the western portal of Britain's longest railway tunnel (excluding underground systems and the Channel Tunnel). Opened by the GWR in 1886 to shorten its route from London to South Wales, the Severn Tunnel was designed by Sir John Hawkshaw (1811–91), is 4 miles 628yd in length and took no fewer than fourteen years to construct. A century later the Second Severn Bridge carrying the M4 motorway was built almost directly above it. (*The Locomotive Publishing Co. Ltd, London*)

Entrance Lock.

New Docks at Avonmouth to be opened by the King in July, 1908.

Where the river ends: Avonmouth, where the Somerset Avon joins the Severn Estuary, which now becomes, technically, the Bristol Channel, leading to the Irish Sea and, beyond that, the North Atlantic. There the waters of the Severn will, in the fullness of time, be evaporated and carried back on the prevailing south-westerly winds to fall as rain on the mountains of Wales, so completing the cycle. This card was produced to mark the visit of Edward VII in July 1908 to open the new King Edward Dock. (*Senior & Co., Bristol*)

During the course of its 220-mile journey through Wales and England,
the Hafren/Severn has dropped almost 2,000ft and drained 4,400 square miles of land.
It has flowed through four counties and three county towns, passed under one hundred
bridges, fed six sets of locks and occasioned the construction of the longest main line railway
tunnel in Britain. In its estuary, its tidal range of up to 52ft is the second highest in the
world. It is, without doubt, the greatest river in the country.